Iowa's Prophetic Journey

Greg Crawford

"Iowa's Prophetic Journey"

All Rights Reserved

Copyrighted 2009 by Greg Crawford

Cover Design by Josh Crawford

No part of this book may be reproduced or transmitted in any form or by any means, graphic, electronic or mechanical, including photocopying, recording, taping, or by any information storage retrieval system, without written permission in writing from the author. The use of short quotes or occasional copying for group study is permitted. All scripture is King James Version

Published by:

Creative Release Publishing

Des Moines, Iowa

thebaseiowa.org

Printed in the United States

First printing 2009

Second Printing 2017

ISBN – 978-1481207416

Contents

Introduction

The Iowa Band .... Page 9

Iowa Alliance State Travels .... Page 19

Current Prophetic Words .... Page 63
    Greg Austin   Page 63
    Dutch Sheets   Page 64
    Chuck Pierce   Page 70
    Dutch Sheets   Page 72
    Chuck Pierce   Page 81
    Cindy Jacobs   Page 83
    Greg Crawford   Page 83
    Bob Newton   Page 85
    Greg Crawford   Page 86
    Cindy Jacobs   Page 89

The Four Anointings for Iowa .... Page 95

Not Abandoning Our Prophetic Journey……………………. Page 137

The Journey Continues (New) ……. Page 141

New Prophetic Words ……………….. Page 143

    New Birth of Freedom Page 143

    Burning the Religious Cornfields Page 148

    Building a Throne in Iowa Page 149

    Extending Boundaries Page 163

    Fire from Within Page 164

    Crossing Borders Page 169

    Visitation for Iowa Page 174

    Iowa is Iona Page 178

About The Author…………..……….. Page 181

Introduction

This book is a simple layout attempting to show the spiritual heritage of the state of Iowa. It is far from all inclusive, but much research has gone into it. Many of the references are out of print and in some cases the only remaining copy is in the possession of Jubilee International Ministries. Many of the things written here can also be found on the Ministry Base web site at
www.thebaseiowa.org

After reading what occurred and what has been prophetically spoken over Iowa, you will see we are a state full of promise and favor with God. This state, like so many others, was founded with Christian roots and principles. Some of this is still in place but we have lost sight of others. This book is an endeavor to revisit some of these ancient promises and become refocused so we do not abandon our prophetic journey!

Chapter 1

The Iowa Band

Without going into the spiritual darkness of First Nations and other prior inhabitants, but looking at the actual Christian influences, "The Iowa Band" is the true beginning spiritual heritage of Iowa settlers. The Iowa Band was made up of 12 ministers, all trained at Andover Theological Seminary, who agreed to carry the gospel into a frontier region. The twelve original prospective home missionaries were Daniel Lane (leader of the Keosauqua Academy where he stayed and trained young people), Harvey Adams, Erastus Ripley, Horace Hutchinson, Alden B. Robbins. William Salter(started Iowa College), Edwin B. Turner, Benjamin A. Spaulding (stationed in Muscatine), William Hammond, James J. Hill (Missionary to Mt. Pleasant), Ebenezer Aiden, Ephraim Adams (scribe) and C.E. Brown who came earlier in the Maquoketa area. (Bates was an Iowa native that joined.)

The Iowa Band set out with the mission to establish God's Glory and His Word in the Beauty of His Holiness. The spirit with which these home missionaries went forth was ably expressed by one of the Iowa Band when he said: "The understanding is among us all, that we go west not for a temporary purpose, unless the great Head of the Church shall make it so. We go to remain permanently -- to live and die there -- and God grant us grace to carry out this purpose."

The group arrived in 1843, and each minister selected a different town in which to establish a congregation. Many stayed in the above mentioned towns while others continued on west past Iowa into Kansas and Nebraska. Out of the 12 men, 5 were apostles and prophets, and 2 of them oversaw and pushed forward the work of God (Brown and Bates). The Iowa Band's motto was "each a church; all a college."

After a number of years when each minister worked independently, the ministers collectively helped to establish Iowa College in Davenport. Later church officials moved the college to Grinnell and changed its name to Grinnell College. The letters and journal of William Salter, a member of the Iowa Band, depict the commitment and philosophy of this small group. At one point, Salter wrote the following to his fiancée back East: "I shall aim to show that the West will be just what others make it, and that they which work the hardest and do the most for it shall have it. Prayer and pain will save the West and the Country is worth it, 'Let God arise, let his enemies be scattered'. " The Iowa Band is also known as the most influential group of leaders in the reformation of 1830-1900. They alone were the group of individuals that established the reformation in Iowa.

While attending Lyman Beecher's Church (Charles Finney's Church in Oberlin, OH) in 1842, 5 of the 11 men received a prophecy that was the mandate of the Puritans and God's purpose for America. Beecher prophesied," if this nation is, in the providence of God, destined to lead the way in moral and political emancipation of the world; it is time she understood her high calling, and was harnessed for the work." First one had to recognize that "it is equally plain that the religious and political destiny of our nation is to be decided in the West and hinges on Iowa. There is the territory, and there will soon be the population, the wealth, and the political power. Whatever we do, it must be done quickly; for there is a tide in human things which waits not -- moments on which the destiny of a nation balances, when the light dust may turn the right way or the wrong. And such is the condition of our nation now. Mighty influences are bearing on us and a slight effort now may secure what ages of repentance cannot remove away. We must reveal the Kingdom to the whole nation while we may. All who are alive must be enlightened, and reached by the restraining and preserving energies of heaven." This is the beginning of the great promises and mandates upon Iowa as a state. We can see many of these things have occurred. Iowa leads the nation in agriculture and is the first in the nation with political caucuses. They said we would be an example of morality. This is currently trying to slide from our grasp. So the question is, have we held the ground?   These 5 men took that confirmation of the call and with Beecher's laying on of hands, went to Iowa in 1843, they set apart in a school in Keosauqua, and set out for the NE corner to establish, " God's Living Word in the hearts of all men".

In 1845, 3 of the 5 men of the Iowa Band moved on further to the West, the reasons were for either God or gold, leaving 2 men to establish what God purposed in this great land; Charles E Brown, and John Bates, an apostle and prophet team.

In 1846-1857 - New leaders arose in Iowa. Bates and Brown established Maquoketa as an Antioch Resource center for all 'passing through' missionaries and preachers. Iowa was beginning to have the reputation of being a land where, "the evidence and the power of the Word and Spirit of God is, to awaken the conscience and lead men into all truth". It was a land of bounty. When the Iowa Band first arrived in the state, they made a covenant with the land itself and claimed it as God's provision. Artists traveled to the 'beautiful land between two rivers' to capture the creativity of God to display to others. Iowa was blossoming under the hand of God and His chosen leaders.

A revival broke out in 1857, at Strawberry Point. Eye witness accounts state, "some remarkable manifestations of Divine power, not only in conversions, but in leading converts to scriptural views of His Kingdom and ordinances". It began a season of salvation releasing a year of unusual revival and prosperity. In one meeting alone, there were over 600 salvations and baptisms similar to the Book of Acts where fire and tongues occurred in the currently still unpopulated areas. Many converts experiencing this were Native Americans. The reformation was under way reaching those thought to be unreachable. The Spirit was moving in an unprecedented way. Almost all the churches of the state were connected in an alliance. They shared Sunday school type materials and exchanged pulpits. They sent help when needed and worked together to see the Kingdom come. At this time, Waterloo was only around 75 families large with a population of around 375 people. Almost all were converted. But the people of Iowa were at the point of decision. Civil war was on the horizon. Iowa was somewhat distanced from it but was still feeling the pressure to participate. The Church was also at a crucial point of decision. Prophet Bates addressed every denomination and leader in the state at the time; "Brethren, we need more of the Spirit of God, more of a Missionary spirit, individual zeal, and enlarged benevolence in sustaining Sabbath Schools, and a better support could and ought to be given by the churches to those ministers who labor in word and doctrine. Let us take heed that we are not absorbed too much in war. We are Christians as well as patriots. The first honor is to be self-denying and ready to die as martyrs in the cause of Christ; the next honor is to be self-denying and ready to die as patriots in the cause of our country."

The Church in Iowa never made that decision. Instead of embracing martyrdom, they embraced causes of social and personal injustices, rather than Kingdom advancement. Ministry to the natives stopped and so did Ministry to the Lord. The structure and their functions changed into man's purposes. Affections in the hearts of the people shifted as well. Iowa entered a stage of politics and growth without the plans of God as a corporate unified Church believing political means were the answer. Men's agendas began to take hold, and the covenants of the pioneers and the Iowa Band were soon forgotten due to war with God's purpose and war with brothers (Civil War). The tight knit alliance was soon disbanded and ministers were "on their own".

Few know, but a Mr. Robert Parham from Muscatine, was in this meeting of discussing the future. Robert had a desire to see Iowa become the place of God's glory like so many others that were touched by the mandate of God. He had experienced these early outpourings of the Spirit. Robert had a son named Charles. Charles looked at the state of the Church in Iowa and how they had rejected following God's revelation for them. He moved to Kansas thinking that perhaps further West from the divided nation and in a new territory he could have expression of his beliefs. Charles Parham is the father of the Pentecostal movement. He taught William Seymour through a doorway in his Bible school in Kansas. Seymour then moved to Azusa Street and the Pentecostal movement was birthed.

Iowa missed her prophetic destiny as the creative land of God between the two rivers, often called the living waters, to have the purpose of the baptism of the Holy Spirit being restored to the Church. But that was not the whole purpose. As we know, the whole purpose was to establish a land of creativity and training so the Glory of God and His Living Word would go forth to all nations!

1859 - Marked the year of destitution as C. Brown states, "It has been a year of very limited spiritual fruitage, and great destitution, the Church has fallen asleep". Churches were burned and the outreach to the Native Americans ceased due to war. The Church lost its cause of martyrdom and the Kingdom, and chose the cause of patriotism. Politics entered the Church in NE Iowa, and hope became deferred. Innocent blood was shed in war and pride. Darkness and sleep entered the Church. Let us not miss our current prophetic destiny as a state!

The Iowa Band started with a mandate from scripture. Amazingly, as a ministry, we preached this mandate 2 years prior to finding out the information on the Iowa Band. We also traveled most of the routes the band traveled over 1 year conducting reformation meetings. God desires us to pick up the mantle of reformation once spoken over our state and see it come to pass.

The Iowa band came with the mandate of Isaiah 25:6-7, and Isaiah 2:2-3:

Isaiah 25:6-7
6 And in this mountain shall the LORD of hosts make unto all people a feast of fat things, a feast of wines on the lees, of fat things full of marrow, of wines on the lees well refined.
7 And he will destroy in this mountain the face of the covering cast over all people, and the veil that is spread over all nations.

Isaiah 2:2-3
2 And it shall come to pass in the last days, that the mountain of the LORD's house shall be established in the top of the mountains, and shall be exalted above the hills; and all nations shall flow unto it.
3 And many people shall go and say, Come ye, and let us go up to the mountain of the LORD, to the house of the God of Jacob; and he will teach us of his ways, and we will walk in his paths: for

out of Zion shall go forth the law, and the word of the LORD from Jerusalem.

What the Iowa Band established:

- Oberlin College (Ohio) 1842
- Iowa College 1846
- University of Northern Iowa 1845
- Grinnell College 1859
- First Christian State Convention 1845
- Over 600 churches
- 200 schools and Bible classes
- A sending center at the church in Maquoketa 1845
- Organized the civil government in Burlington and Iowa City and Des Moines
- Established a sending and training center for young people in Keosauqua, Denmark, Maquoketa, Burlington, and Muscatine. 1845 - 1857
- Trained nearly 10,000 missionaries and leaders for the cause of Christ to go further west.
- All in a 12 year span of time

A complete history of the Iowa band can be found at www.iowaalliance.org . At this site, is the complete book the Iowa Band wrote concerning their work.

Greg Crawford

This book is in downloadable PDF files scanned from the last remaining copy in print.

Chapter 2

Iowa Alliance for Reformation

The Iowa Alliance for Reformation emerged under God's divine direction to release revelation into the state of Iowa and bring reformation into the Church. The Lord spoke specifically to the leadership here at Jubilee International Ministries in Fairfield Iowa - if we would clean the slate, God would change the state within two years. We cancelled all overseas travel, restructured the entire ministry focus, and for the next 2 years focused only on Iowa. God put it in our hearts to travel county to county and conduct Reformation meetings releasing creative flow and revelation through worship, to encourage existing leaders to pursue Revelation, and to cause the Body of Christ of Iowa to hunger for greater encounters with God.

As we started this journey into our prophetic destiny, we also found out the great parallels we are reliving. We had 5 men start the Iowa Alliance for Reformation and only 2 remained to travel and complete the assignment as well. We started from Fairfield, located in SE Iowa and traveled almost the same path as the Iowa Band. What is amazing is we did not uncover the Iowa Band information until half way through our prophetic journey. It confirmed many things. I was given a 1900 tent stake as a prophetic act by our Bible students to make covenants with the land by staking it wherever we go. So did the Iowa Band make covenant. I spoke at a conference in Oberlin, Ohio the place of Charles Finney's church. When I visited the church and stood behind Charles Finney's pulpit, God said, " You are going to take the spirit of reformation that is here back to Iowa to fulfill". I considered what was said and wondered exactly what it meant. A year later after we had started traveling the state, we came across the Iowa Band Prophecy that occurred at the exact spot I stood and received the word of the Lord.

As the Iowa Alliance was formed and began to function, we would send letters to churches and groups inviting them in a 5-6 county area for meetings. It was not about the numbers that showed but God said what we would release into the spiritual realm over each area. The notes and details of the intercession that occurred weeks leading into and prior to a meeting are enormous and for this writing only the actual Alliance meetings themselves are documented. We would conduct spiritual history and intercede with factual knowledge. Then we would travel into the area with our entire apostolic company of forty+ trained and ready.

Prophetic and creative worship was the primary focus along with revelatory teaching. We built relationships with leaders hungry for more and desiring to see a true reformation come into the Church. For two years, after coming through a place, testimonies still came in telling of the shift over the spiritual realm that occurred. We may not have seen the results at the moment but we can now say after completing the assignment we have seen the change God said would occur.

A total of twelve meetings were held. This number was just the way it came and ended, not planned or tried to make happen. Twelve is the number for government and until I actually sat down to compile this writing, I did not realize that is what occurred! Almost all the meeting halls and expenses were paid by those we traveled with out of their own pocket as an act of obedience. God placed a state within the hearts of the forty+ who faithfully gave their time.

The Iowa Alliance for Reformation Council

Coming out of the state regional meetings, a need to have a state council was evident. Also revealed was the great potential and resources within the Church with the need for direction, mobilization, and affirmation of the existing emerging apostolic companies within the state. Somehow the state needed to connect. The Iowa Council for Reformation was birthed in the spring of 2008 under the divine inspiration of the Holy Spirit. After talking with many, the need of the formation of this council was coming to bear. In the spring of 2008, Greg Crawford, along with others from the state of Iowa, attended a conference in Colorado Springs to launch the United States Alliance for Reformation under Dutch Sheets and Robert Henderson's leadership. Dutch mentioned the need for state wide apostolic counsels to be formed to mobilize the Body of Christ. Upon returning from this trip, he called for a gathering of leaders and ministries to be formed for the first time within the state. The willingness to come to together was great from the beginning and all looked at this as an opportunity to advance the Kingdom of God together doing what no one person could do, to create something of such magnitude it would touch every person in the state. From that point forward, this council had moved in amazing harmony and willingness to serve each other and the emerging leaders of Iowa. This council was also approved and commissioned under Dutch Sheets' United States Alliance for Reformation (USAR). Greg Crawford of J.I.M. Ministry Base had been approved as the State coordinator for the USAR for Iowa. (Editor's note: It was later decided by Dutch Sheets to drop the USAR since other national groups were already in existence.)

Iowa Alliance for Reformation meetings

The Reformation meetings occurred over the course of two years and twelve locations. Invitations were sent out to almost all churches within a region and the event was only one afternoon. The following is a brief overview of these meetings

Keosauqua Fall 2006

The alliance meeting started out in the small town of Keosauqua, Iowa in the southeast corner of the state. It was not really advertised as an alliance meeting, but as a worship gathering to be held in the city park. This first meeting only had a handful of people in attendance due to a home football game scheduled the same night. With the small turnout, it would have been easy to be discouraged. After all, we brought all our sound equipment and gear for this event. We pressed through the night knowing that what we were doing and declaring would have an effect over the city whether anyone was present or not. The small crowd enabled us to make more intense declarations over the region speaking openly about the things that were holding so many people back.

Much later after this first meeting was held, we found out it was the exact same city the Iowa band came through when they first entered the state. As a matter of fact, in this small city of 2500 people or less, the Iowa band had established its first Bible school that the reformers were sent from into the rest of the state. It would be over a year later before we realized that this prophetic act was the beginning of our group repeating almost the same route the Iowa band had taken.

Kalona, Feb. 2007 planning meeting

After conducting the first meeting in Keosauqua, the need to formally organize the Iowa Alliance for Reformation was soon realized. An informal gathering of 5 ministry leaders was held in Kalona. We all came into agreement of the need of the Reformation meetings and the need to travel throughout the state of Iowa. There was also much discussion about the need for all of us to lay down our own lives and ministries and make the state of Iowa a priority. From this meeting of five, we soon realized that only two would complete the assignment, Prophet Gerald Knock of Tiffin, Iowa and Apostle Greg Crawford of Fairfield, Iowa. Once again, like the Iowa band, five started on the assignment and two finished. We repeated this same story in modern-day times.

Rev. Gerald Knock Apostle Greg Crawford

Pella, Iowa   Feb. 2007

The first scheduled alliance meeting was held in Pella, Iowa. Many prayers and relationship building had already taken place in this city by much time spent there by the Jubilee International Ministries Ministry Base. It was decided that this would be the most appropriate place for an official launch. Plans were underway and as the appointed evening approached, one of the worst snowstorms of that winter also approached. The determination to not allow anything to get in the way of fulfilling this mandate for the state was evident. We loaded our gear and started out before the worst of the storm had hit. I told everyone we are going up together as one and returning together as one. Not caring what we would do afterwards or how we would make a 90-mile trip home, we set off.

When we arrived in Pella at the Vermeer Manufacturing Hall, so did the storm. How fitting to be in a facility started to glean the fields of Iowa, producing the first large round hay bailer. We set up our sound equipment in faith and believed that God would bring those who had a heart for the state. Some people traveled in almost blizzard conditions of blowing and drifting snow for this amazing event. Some drove as far away as 100 miles taking hours to arrive. Amazing when you have a mandate from the Lord! Equally amazing was the fact that local people who had planned on coming could not make the short distance.

The worship service began with excitement and anticipation of the beginning of creating history. Josh Crawford, our worship leader declared "Marching orders are going forth this night". Prophetic songs and worship unfolded and prophetic decrees were issued. One song in particular was sung at this first official meeting. It had just been written by Josh Crawford entitled "Terrible With Banners" a song about God's army marching through the land. Unknown to Josh, two years later he would sing this song again at the last Alliance meeting.

Pella snow storm at Vermeer Complex

  A prophetic word was given that the churches in the region would feel the effect of this night within seven days and within three weeks things would shift. God declared He would apply pressure upon leaders for change. The Lord was more concerned about the small places of men's hearts He was building than the large structures men were building. We declared we were building the Tabernacle of the Lord within the State of Iowa. He was going to remove the structures that did not allow His fullness to come. The Spirit of the Lord then spoke and said ***"To Reasonor: fire, vengeance. To Baxtor: coming for ones left behind. To Grinnell: heart. To Searsboro: My Spirit burns, not forsaken. To Tracey: not in dark places, the church structures will not hold when I expand. To Pleasantville: I am coming. Hearts of these areas, destitute ones. Multitude poor in*** *spirit, Daniels, Josephs to feed them. A nation shall be brought forth. Many are looking for you to lead forth. Much is at stake this hour. MY people there are new dimensions in lives, new walk in a new season. My purpose, My identity is in it. I've tried you and hid you. Dry yet able to endure. To the Remnant hidden in caves and mountains they are coming out. The season is victory in heart, ordained of Me in this hour. Come into that I've called you forth. My voice in your ears. Be My voice, My sound. Release into hearts of many. Release what's inside you."*

Then the word of the Lord came strongly through me. *"I come with the sting of a hornet, the hornet of my anger, the anger of Jealousy < for what I have invested, I have invested much into ... Not to destroy, but to get men's attention. The Jebusites, and the Hittites will not stand. Deal with hearts of men, not like in the past, to carry the anointing of Repentance of the Land, to carry... The sting: 1st the leaders, 2nd the people. The season declaring and coming, removing obstacles, your mouth will carry the sting in it, shift in mindset > effects your heart. It is the shift in your heart that concerns me tonight. It shall sting, it shall sting. It shall keep coming to change men's mindsets, but shall not destroy. I'm coming to bring inheritance of the Land. Do not be distracted, do not be distracted. It shall be passed to the next generation. Three generations* *touch what I'm doing in this hour. That is My heart this night."*

There was also the revealing of false prophets working within the land. Bringing words of comfort and entertaining men's hearts instead of confronting them. The word of the Lord came again, ***"The shift comes when the trumpet of gathering is ended over the state. When all brethren called, will come. Angels are in the night sky in Iowa. Like fireflies in the night, fiery beams lighting up the vials, releasing a residue. It is a famine hour, manna fell only for a time and season. You do not want to see what grieves Me.***
Do you see what I see that grieves My heart?"

Prophetic Artwork Drawn during the meeting by Katie Lauer.   Entitled : "Victory Dance"

It was decreed that the Midwest has reached the verge of going beyond what God will allow. This Woe is not God's judgment but God's mercy to save us because God's people are so hungry. Leaders cannot compromise anymore to what men want, they must speak out of heaven with no fear of men, and must stand against the onslaught. See ones standing with them in integrity and righteousness. Standing in holiness.

It was also spoken that Pella means a mountain of refuge, and that four counties are refuge counties. It was spoken that we would see three signs in the Church, three generations with the fullness of the seven-fold Spirit descending with everything! ***"You will see the thing of Ananias and Sapphira, and I will raise it up! The head is falling down; the young are standing up on it. Get yourself up to the place. The ladder is open! The steps are open! Jacob saw the fullness of it, and this fullness starts here in Pella. It's a different dynamic, there is a different weight on this new thing; a mantle of responsibility. You've got to take on the weight, the call then reformation will come."***

Several saw a large spider in the spirit with its legs in the four counties. Others shared dreams and visions. There was much sharing about Jezebel and how the spirit had so manipulated the men of God within our state. God had prepared the people for this night to come forth with insights. We concluded the meeting by announcing to "Dance the Dance of Miriam. A victory dance!" We danced and celebrated beyond our allotted time in the building.

The reports came back in eight days of a new prophetic flow in worship that had broken out in one of the large Dutch reformed churches. This was something new to them that they had not experienced.

As the meeting came to a close, so did the snowstorm. We loaded our gear and hit the road to find out the snow plows were ahead of us. We were able to go home at 50 mph right after a major Iowa storm. We had fulfilled the assignment and had shifted the heavens. We were on the way to change the state!

Burlington March 07

The spirits were high for the meeting in Burlington. Spring had come and there was a great freshness in the air. The promise of a large turnout seemed at hand for the meeting. After all, some pastors said they were coming. It was even being promoted in one church in the region. We rented a large hall and anticipated something was about to happen.

But what did happen was the turnout was small, but those who came had encounters with God. The meeting started by the Lord saying ***"Awake! Sin not! This is the Day I longed for, I brought you to this place. Church Arise, Awake! Come out of that sleep, that slumber! To the spiritually dead, I say: hear it"***

Pastor Selman from Burlington spoke, "this last hour God has been shaking things up. What was not built on solid ground but on sand, will be shifted! Reconciliation in the Body of Christ is needed and God is doing a new thing in Southeast Iowa. This last hour confirmed things in my spirit, we must be of one mind, of one accord, and God will do what He said."

Then the Lord spoke *"**Miracles will come to pass upon these counties, as shifting here starts. In seven weeks fullness will come. A seven-fold anointing of My Son. Newness, freshness shall surely come**"* It seemed the word given was also conditional if the Church would step out and step into what the Spirit was doing.

"Iowa's Prophetic Journey"

Artwork drawn during the meeting by Katie Lauer. She was inspired by the ministry to a Pastor as Apostle Greg Crawford held him in his arms as he wept.

I gave a word to one pastor about how he was about to quit and how God had sent us here for him. I held him in my arms as he wept and said he had wondered if his life counted and if he would ever see a move of God. He said "this you have showed me today is what I have waited my whole life for". God was amazing in how he honored the few who came.

This meeting also had prophetic words concerning timing, flooding, and the dams of the Mississippi as a sign of God flooding his four anointings into the state. (See chapter on this) The word came to pass just as the Lord said months later with the exact dam and the four rivers spoken of. But the main word given was that God was calling our state to holiness and as the heart of the nation so would the nation go. That as Burlington was a type of port city exporting grain to the nation and world and God wanted to use it to export revelation to the nation.

I had to encourage our people that this was not about numbers, but about the mandate we had been given. There was much dealing with hearts in this moment. Some now would begin to fall off from our own group of trained warriors. It could not matter we had a promise to see fulfilled.

Muscatine June 2007

As we went to Muscatine, our attitudes were different we knew we were on a divine mission. We rented a motel meeting room and gathered about a hundred people.

The Lord spoke ***"Iowa awakening is coming. Muscatine Community College what you voice will be established over Muscatine"***

I saw release of apostolic authority in Muscatine church leaders. ***"Arise in this hour, connect with the Government of God for Word and Power."***

It was revealed that we as a group had been in a forming process. In Pella, we were worshippers. In Burlington, we were warriors. And now in Muscatine, we were truly reformers. It was a test to see if we would reform without looking back. The Lord then said **"I place a Seal upon hearts into deepening of who you are! Holy remnant you're not forgotten. Hear! This is the place and time. "**

It was spoken how from this place the reformers would come forth. Those setting in unrest and searching out the Lord's voice in Iowa for Iowa. The unrest would continue in hearts until reformation was done. God was moving on hearts. It is no wonder because Muscatine was also key to the Iowa Band as well. We declared that vision is restored in this place. To the Holy remnant all that matters are the promises. Then this prophetic song came forth.

"I'm bringing My Breath into you

   Will you take this?

   Will you receive now?

   Because I am creating now

   A new sharp threshing instrument

   I am creating now

   A breath that's everlasting,

Like a fire I will burn

I am breathing out into you!

My Breath will burn into your lungs,

I'll breathe into you a new creation

Muscatine is pressing into Me now

Receive this grace now

*I'm putting on you, **GRACE***

There's a new threshing instrument"

Muscatine Alliance Meeting

As the Lord showed us, we began to call forth reformers. I called out one man in particular who had just moved here from Brazil. He had been part of the Argentine revival and had pastored in a large church. The Lord told him to move his family to Iowa because he was about to do something big in the area of reformation. Many were encouraged. We then focused on intercessors and ministry to them specifically. One pastor in particular was greatly encouraged and to this day speaks of that meeting changing his entire ministry. He still gives reports that he can look back and see how this one meeting shifted events in his region. We left with this one thought: 'You've chosen us as the Warriors, Worshippers, Reformers! To make history once again.'

Creston   Aug. 2007

At Creston, Pastor Jim McCutchan who held the ground in a very hard place hosted us. His group of believers rented the motel meeting room. We began the meeting 3 ½ hours from home. Not only was the spiritual battle difficult going into this, but my family was going through much personal hardship as well. The people there could not believe we had come so far. We were a little amazed ourselves, but knew the NW corner of the state was going to take a real commitment to follow through with. This seemed to be a testing but everyone was happy to pay such a small price for such a large honor.

Pastor Jim McCutchan and Josh Crawford

The worship was very exuberant. Dancing went on for a long time with expressions with flags and banners. It was a great joy to see the older ones dancing alongside the younger. Worship was also prophetic. The main focus of this meeting was how the older generation had held on for years for breakthrough and promise and how they had become weary. The message came from Ps. 126.

Psalm 126 When the LORD turned again the captivity of Zion, we were like them that dream . [2] Then was our mouth filled with laughter, and our tongue with singing: then said they among the heathen, The LORD hath done great things for them. [3] The LORD hath done great things for us; whereof we are glad . [4] Turn again our captivity, O LORD, as the streams in the south . [5] They that sow in tears shall reap in joy . [6] He that goeth

forth and weepeth, bearing precious seed, shall doubtless come again with rejoicing, bringing his sheaves with him.

Creston gathering

Young generation infusing strength into the Jacob dreamers

The Lord spoke **"This is the gate of heaven, like Jacob wrestled for the blessing so have you. You have wrestled for the blessing so the next generation can receive it!"**

Worship and Creative Flow

The decree was that the harvest desired would surely come in because of the weeping that had occurred. They were asked how many had held on for over 25 years. Many hands went up, actually an uncommon number than what you would ever expect. The Lord spoke ***"For your great suffering you shall have great reward."*** There was an anointing for the next generation to impart youth and strength into those who had held on for so long. It was decreed they would obtain joy and gladness of heart. That the dream in their hearts was not lost and they needed to dream again. This was about the restoration of dreams lost! The Next Generation imparted under such a strong anointing that some were completely overwhelmed by God's presence. Hope was renewed and a connection between generations occurred. Pastor McCutchan was taken by surprise and greatly encouraged. Even though he had been in an isolated place, God had connected him to something bigger.

He now serves on the Iowa Alliance Council.

Waterloo, Oct 2007

The 2 ½ hour journey to Waterloo seemed short in comparison to Creston. We held the meeting in the IHOPE ministry building, the local house of prayer and free medical clinic. We were surprised to see people from prior Alliance meetings come to this one as well. It seemed God had put the state of Iowa in the hearts of others after seeing what we were doing. This meeting seemed to take a deeper vein than others.

Waterloo release of creative miracles!

Worship took on a time of excitement and celebration. Great joy was present that caused some who had never danced to be supernaturally caught away in it. It was as if everyone was truly celebrating from the heart and from these excited hearts, the expression was released. Oil came from our hands for the first time in an Alliance meeting during worship. We had experienced this at other times but never on the road. For the first time on the road we also heard angels singing with us in the meeting. The angelic singing was heard not by one or two but by many! We were in another realm for sure and had established a tremendous portal to heaven.

The Lord said ***"Seeds of Righteousness are born, Heaven and earth collide, Power & Force join in a unique way. There is a Creative flow. My mind will be made known. My children will bring life more abundantly. My Spirit is brooding as you co-labor. I will bring rest and turn mourning into gladness. Receive freedom from my hands. Come closer, deeper, I want you."***

Waterloo -where we heard angels sing!

Who will go and lay down lives daily? Setting aside their dreams for My dreams. To be carriers of My glory. Who will pay the price as Reformers? My Spirit changes old mind sets. I come quickly. Press into Me. Spend more time with Me. I want to adorn you with more."

The Lord said *"No more struggling, no more wandering. Believe I need Reformers to be Face to Face with me. A mandate is given to you this day. Will you pray? Will you go? Who is the King of Glory? The mighty One, like a Man of War? I say Resurrection Light, New Beginnings to you, things are new this day. Complete today, complete the circle. Reformers are coming with power, with anointing, to conquer strongholds"*

We decreed the breaking of the portal of poverty that rested over the region. We loosed the realms of possibilities in the Lord. We closed demonic activity and spoke life over the North East corner of Iowa, which affects Des Moines, flows to the center of the state. We broke the spirit of death, and released the flow of Life. We decreed the reformers to come out of hiding, let them come forth in Jesus' name!

People were called forward to answer the call as reformers again. We laid hands on them and released the spirit of the reformer upon them. Then a second call was made for healings and miracles. We knew God would answer, after all, we still had oil dripping from our hands. Miracles also started to occur with many healings and one person had a heart valve replaced. His doctor canceled his operation and told him to come back in a year for a checkup! The Lord was confirming this Kingdom assignment now with miracles.

"Iowa's Prophetic Journey"

Des Moines   Dec. 2007

Capitol Cities Governmental Prayer

Though not officially an Alliance meeting, the Capitol Cities meeting with Dr. Hope Taylor looked very much like an Alliance meeting. We gathered prayer groups from around the area and went to the capitol to pray. We prayed in the House of Representatives visitor balcony for almost an hour. We returned to a borrowed church sanctuary and continued the meeting. It was almost an all day event. We made decrees over our state and nation. We warred in the Spirit for our country. The Lord moved mightily in our midst as we could feel the shift in the atmosphere over the capitol city change.

Prayer in the Iowa House of Representatives

Ottumwa, Jan. 2008

Since Ottumwa was close to us and within our region, we held three very focused intercession sessions for this event. After all, we were in our home region where a lot of people knew who we were. We purposely held off the closer places until the dead of winter and we had completed meetings further out.

We set up at the Bridge View Convention Center. A new facility with plenty of room and probably the best venue we used in all of the state traveling. Ottumwa is called the 'city of bridges'.

Ottumwa, Portal of Miracles

The Lord spoke and said ***"This City of Bridges, a Bridge into heaven, into My very heart. It holds multiple facts and dynamics of Me. A new anointing is on this city, it is a portal of My Presence. Different anointings are to be seen. Within three weeks, a shifting, an increase. Angels descend and ascend, and will visit this city again after 25 years of people seeing them. They shall know, I will bring My messengers from afar, see My heart as it bridges into this city, My very heart and My throne."***

The Spirit was brooding over the entire meeting to create and release. The Lord spoke and said "***A Restoration, A Reformation, today, and the pattern for this year.***"

Artwork drawn by Katie Lauer during the meeting. She was inspired as she saw and heard the Lord say "I am imparting my heart to you".

    I shared from *2 Chronicles 34* and how Josiah at 8 years old became a reformer and changed a nation. I challenged those in attendance of the Iowa Band and how a 150 year old mandate still rests on us to train reformers and send them into the nation. I said the reformation container is already here, it is being identified, purified and brought into holiness.

The Josiahs are ready to be put into place. God wants us in a place of tension. Josiah burned the idols, tension! Baal's prophets were burned, tension! If we refuse to bow to man's stuff, we shall shift much. God is about to release Reformation (restructure), Messengers (to declare). Reformation is coming for our nation's sake. Reformation comes from "Nobodies." We can be like Josiah, used by God, doing signs, wonders, and miracles.

We then prayed over names for salvation that had been placed in a large fish net. The anointing hit some so hard they could not leave the net even as the meeting moved forward.

Stroke Victim totally healed

There appeared a visible portal on the stage with miracles in it. I could see them swirling. Oil was dripping from my hands as well. I challenged the people to come forward into this portal if they needed a miracle. No one moved. It seemed foreign to everyone that such a thing could exist. I encouraged them again and people came running on the second invitation. Prophetic words began, healing occurred and miracles came forth like water running from a tap.

We called forth the reformers again and many answered the call. Several pastors came forward as well. I spoke to a pastor and released a word to him "It is not about the assignment but about the reformation" (three weeks later he was voted out of his church which caused those who remained to take a hard look at things and shifted their mindset) Several received healings. We prayed for a stroke victim who received total healing and restored feeling on the left side. Another healing was a severely crushed ankle and the cast was taken off in the next couple of days.

The Ottumwa meeting seemed to have all the dynamics of reformation in it. Miracles, healings, open heaven, revelatory truth, prophetic and creative flow and the challenge of reformation. The pattern of these meetings was taking shape.

Grinnell, May 2008

The meeting in Grinnell was especially exciting for us. Now knowing the history of the Iowa Band, our expectation for the meeting was very high. The meeting did not open with typical worship decrees or teaching. It opened with prophetic utterance as if the Lord was picking up where the Iowa Band left off.

Josh Crawford, our worship leader, opened the meeting with a prophetic word, I hear the Lord saying, *"This will be a place of refuge and of gathering. It is a habitation of the glory of the King. A place for training in how to usher in a Kingdom for a King. This will be a place of refreshing for the wounded ones, they will be coming. This will be a place set apart for the King. The former rain is past and the latter rain has begun in Grinnell. There are some things formed, but the latter things must come. Even in the training on this very campus there is a new and living thing. The latter things are birthed in the Spirit. Until the day I return, you will enter into latter rain. The Underground Railroad was in this place. The latter thing I'm bringing is like this a place of refuge. A place to feed the hungry. You'll raise up a mighty voice. You'll legislate refuge to those who set policy in the land. These are the latter things you'll govern. The Spirit of adoption is here in this place. I'm reclaiming My righteous ones who will stand in the house and legislate. You must settle the day, former things done, latter things begun. "*

Then another word was released through Steve Walz, *"A release of epic proportions. This is a place of rest, a cup of refreshing water. The cup size you bring to the altar determines how much you receive. Freely receive. You can only carry what you have made room for.*
Will you draw close? Are you willing to be a reformer? To exchange your life for the many? For those who answer, much will be given."

The Lord then spoke through me and said *"Grinnell, a City of Refuge; 1 of 6 in the state where His Presence will dwell. I say it is settled"*

We then entered into worship. It became very militant and we began to make decrees. Then I encouraged everyone "Grinnell is where the Iowa Band put a dollar on the table and believed God for the rest to build the three colleges in Iowa they started. Grinnell seems to be a key starting point. It was declared by the Iowa Band to be a mountain of the Lord. Isaiah 2:2-3, Mountain of God established, His House built up on top. Grinnell was to be a place of the vantagepoint. The people were exhorted to not be concerned about it not showing forth instantaneously, but to work for the long result. In **Isaiah 25:1-3**, we see a ruined city and the need for a refuge city. God wants a mountain here to bring justice. **Isaiah 25:10**, the Lord's hand rests on this mountain. Build for three to four generations out. People are coming for God's Presence is going to dwell. There is a Governmental Mantle here today; we must govern the Kingdom! A mandate on Iowa, a place of training Reformers in the nation; Grinnell. The mandate for the state shifts from Grinnell onward."

I then turned to my people and told them "More was going to be required of them in the future. Much more and God would make a demand upon them to sacrifice greater. There will be decisions you must make. There's an anointing placed upon you to carry reformation. Only say what the Father is saying, only do what the Father is doing!" The weight of this declaration over them was felt by every person in the room. God was calling us out now for the future.

We then went into deep militant intercession and decrees. We faced the campus and spoke over it for a long time to return back to its ancient roots. We decreed over Grinnell it was indeed a refuge city. We called out the reformers once again and ministered to the women intercessors of Grinnell who had stood for years believing for a move of God to come. The impartation was so deep almost all of us could not stand under the anointing it carried with it.

This one out of all the meetings was probably one of the deepest we had experienced in the area of warring. It seemed as we left the city that Grinnell was a key place in Iowa and the heart of God. God was not letting go of the foundation that was laid and wants it resurrected again to build upon.

Pella, July 2008

A return to Pella was as if God was giving the area a second chance. It seemed somewhat odd to us but we decided teaching was probably really needed. We had five afternoon teaching sessions on reformation and an evening meeting demonstrating what was taught.

We covered "What is Reformation, Passion for Reformation, Maintaining Prophetic Flow, How Reformation Affects the Next Generation, and How Reformation Affects Intercession".

By having a full day, we were able to have intercession on site before the evening meeting. The intercession would contain key things for our future and the future of the state. It was as if God was revealing our destiny to us. We prayed that we would see his Holiness and it was our portion and Melchizedek's portion as well.

It was declared that Pella would unlock Des Moines. A prophetic word came ***"Besiege Des Moines. A center will be established to take the city. It will***

be a place to change generations."

We declared that life and arteries would flow out of Des Moines. Mike Lauer then had a vision of a cloud in Des Moines forming. Light starting to shadow through it and then displacement happened in the state.

I had just gotten back from Oberlin, Ohio. The year before I had spoken at a conference there and the Lord had spoken I would carry the spirit of reformation back from there to Iowa. This time it was revealed to me through a series of meetings with people that when the Iowa Band had come to the state, a high-ranking witch had come as well following them. Knowing the strength of the band, the witch had gone further West and settled in the Creston, Iowa area. The Alliance council members stood and broke the witchcraft over the SW corner of the state. The anointing as we did this was so powerful we barely were able to stand up under it.

We then entered into worship as the evening meeting flowed out of intercession. This prophetic song came forward from Josh Crawford:

" Come with something sovereign

Come with something sacred that no man can claim it"

Then the Word of the Lord came again *"The hour glass is turned over, You have more time to complete this new pattern. Those who feel unplugged, outlets are opened, plugged in. I redeem time. Resurrection power is in your hands. My house will be established sure, like a gate to Des Moines. Come closer, to a higher place in Spirit. Come into place with milk and honey. A place of new domain as conquerors and warriors moving mightily."*

We concluded knowing God's agenda in this hour was to finish the things before us as a state. We would finish our assignment no matter what.

Sioux Center   Sept 2008

The lack of commitment to do or experience anything radical or out of the typical church structure was very evident in the NW corner. This was reflected in the response we got before the meeting by those we contacted and by the attendance. Not one single person came from the region. Here we had traveled with our entire ministry company the distance of almost five hours. But by now, nothing surprised us.

We had rented a large meeting room in the community center. It had all glass walls on both sides overlooking an all glassed-in swimming pool on one side and a hockey arena on the other. A home football game was also going on and probably 2,000 people walked by looking up at us worshipping with flags, banners and dancing before the lord unashamed. It was like God at the end of the travels had elevated us for all to see. The worship literally went to new heights as we basically just enjoyed ourselves in the Lord. But Dutch Sheets had prophesied that out of the NW corner worship would flow even to the center of the state. We were the fulfillment of prophecy.

The decree went forth that "Every Word you've spoken over my life must be fulfilled!" Because a generation is counting on us, even with just us in this room; affecting a multitude.

God said, ***"The Old Bricks are all falling down! It begins tonight, see it clear to Fairfield, 350 miles away!"***

The Lord then spoke through Judges 7 and said ***"The Sword of the Lord was dropping this night in this place. It was the sword of Gideon and the Lord. The Lord's hand is jabbing His sword into this land."***

The Demonic principalities over the region was revealed and confronted. The Religious spirit was very alive and strong within the region. It was shown it had a veil over the region so the people could not embrace Liberty. The Lord then revealed the principalities over the area from Judges 6:20. The gods that were confronted and used this night in the text were Oreb (Raven) and Zeeb (Wolf). Both steal and feed on dead things! As we looked up, in broad bold colors about 15' high on the wall in the swim area next to us was a raven. It was as if God was confirming the people's affections.

The Lord then spoke that the next day we would also face from Judges 6:20, the kings of the area living in Fort Dodge, kings Zebah (Sacrifice, ie – devoted to Moloch, god of fire; victim, slaughter) & Zalmunna (shadow is withheld; a moving shadow; withdrawn from protection; shelter is denied). The Lord then spoke this word **"Who will bring worship to the North West?"**

He continued through Aissa Ham "isn't there a cause, and to not be afraid of the faces of men." The Lord then said **"Speak my word back to me."**

Sisie Rampengan stood up and said "I have the Kingdom DNA, I want to do this! Take advantage of what God has for you; influence the seven mountains, there is favor and blessing to change the world; to break it open. We have just shown up and God touches the rest, even people in a swimming pool."

Josh Crawford then spoke and said "There are people here in the high place to carry it. We just need to decree all His points of worship! God has positioned people to affect this region! How disappointed He must be today to see no one come; so we worship to create a habitation for You today so creative worship can begin and people FUNCTION here!"

The Word of the Lord came strongly then that the people in the region needed to turn or be in a wrong pattern for 7 years and be the last within the state to break open.
I shared from Ezek. 33:1-7. We had traveled for 2 years giving warning and sounding a trumpet. The Lord said *"You are free from the blood of these. Those not picking up the sound, their own blood is upon them now. I will bless and lead those who respond to the sound."*

For our remembrance, The Lord said *"In five years you will remember this day That I will put tremendous pressure upon North West Iowa, 'til they will give way to this thing of Me. You are free from their blood."*

We finished the meeting in intense worship and a real sense of completion of the far NW corner. We had invited, showed and released God's intentions. We had gleaned the four corners of the state now so that Des Moines must give way. We were ready for the final meeting the next day, heading directly to the center of the state.

Fort Dodge Sept 2008

We traveled back towards home two hours and set all our gear up for the 12th and final time on the two-year assignment. Once again, a small turn out but it did not matter. We had placed over the state of Iowa hundreds of hours of decrees, intercession, worship and prayer. We had the spiritual history of the state and had seen the condition of Iowa in a very true sense. We had gleaned the four corners (Like Ruth gleaning the field) and now the center must give way.

Rev. Knock had seen 'the sword of the Lord' go into the ground in a vision. He had also seen the apostles and prophets going with it. He also saw the team or company of troops we had traveled with go into the ground as well." It would cause judgment and burning because the anointing was there. "

Steve Walz expanded on what was revealed the day before in Sioux Center. He said it was blessing and cursing. The Fear of Man was the spirit Oreb and the fear of Religious Spirits was Zeeb.

It was revealed to us that Fort Dodge was the foundation city of Northwest Iowa. It was like the governmental opening point of the entire region. This explains the revealing of the kings being in this city.

The declarations began. "There comes a cloud with a sword here to break off evil. "

" Cut down idols, apostles and prophets filled by God, pastors, teachers, evangelists filled, to rise up and establish the government of God in this city."

"Sure foundations are set in this city, Intercessors functioning in the heavenly realm"

"Sword here to pass judgment and let Justice come up in this city"

"We declare the end of no blessing, of distractions and we cut off the head of kings tonight, you will not take up residence in Ft. Dodge anymore"

The time ended with one word spoken

"Release!" The word came for all present but for us as a ministry especially. Steve Walz came forward and under the anointing as a spiritual son, released me to go to Des Moines. I publicly announced what God had placed in my heart. We had to move the entire ministry to the capitol city because it was going to give way. He had chosen us to fulfill our prophetic journey. We had a heart for the state as He placed it inside us. We packed our gear and started the final 3 hours home. We were about to create history once again.

"Releasing" us to Des Moines

Chapter 3

Current Prophetic Words

The following are some of the most critical words given within Iowa. They are not all inclusive but are looked upon more as what I would call a state level word. Even though many words are given at gatherings within the state, the following are more focused towards the state as a whole. They also are not just making references in a general sense, but are actually very specific in nature. For a complete listing of words over the state visit www.iowaalliance.org .

Prophetic Word by Greg Austin, July 2003

It is I, and no other, that will accomplish this thing. It is I who will do it. My testimony goes before Me. For in the days of old I have been faithful and the thing that I have spoken, I have performed. Know this, that in your hearing this night, you hear the declaration: "Over thee, O' Iowa, shall I wave My banner of Glory." Many shall be astonished and many shall come. Many of you will go. You will take My Glory to the nation and the nation will take My glory to the earth, 'til all the earth is covered with the knowledge of My Glory as the waters cover the sea. For this is the hour! This is the day! I will come to you and you are here this night to become witnesses to the Truth of My Word.

Dutch Sheets Oct. 27, 2003
Transcribed from the Fifty state Tour

And the revelation that begins to flow for here is not just for here, but it's going to influence the nation and the nations. Isn't it amazing, that in little, old, tucked away, Iowa , where nobody would think a whole lot about it, God starts saying, "I'M going to shift what's happening in the Middle East and Iraq from the cornfields of Iowa ." I mean, go figure… Just go figure… But that's what HE said. Either we receive the prophetic word and believe it, or we're just gonna trash it. But that's what HE said. Something is going to happen here that is going to shift things clear over there.

Now, I didn't even associate that thought with what HE said to me today until just now. "I'M about to open the heavens over Iowa …" And I'm tellin' you that much of this has to do with revelation. When revelation begins to open… when the heavens open in this way, EVERYTHING changes! I'm talkin' EVERYTHING CHANGES!

"It all revolves around revelation," because that is the beginning point. We are going to change the heavenlies over Iowa, because we are moving into a new place of revelation. I want to say this to you, and Chuck touched on this, there is a facet of the prophetic anointing of the LORD that is operating here in Iowa. There is another dimension of the prophetic that you have not yet broken through, but we're gonna do some things in the Spirit to help break this state loose into the prophetic realm of the anointing.

What God is saying to us, and for this state, right now, is, "I want to shift things, so that Words from the LORD become prevalent, and there is great break-through in the realm of revelation. The prophetic anointing of MY Spirit... the prophetic anointing of Christ begins to break loose, across this region, to where the Word of the LORD begins to flow like a river. The heavens and the Book are opened."

"Revelation is about to break through into Iowa that is going to change," the LORD said, "the very earth." It's going to change the nation. HE said, "You are going to feed the nation revelation." HE said, "You are going to even feed it into the Middle East , and Iraq is going to change because of decrees from Iowa .I AM about to open the heavens over Iowa . The

"Bread of Heaven" is going to be released in a new way to feed the people of God." We say that the prophetic anointing of God is now being released over Iowa in a way that it's never been released before. We lay hands, as it were, on this region. And we say, "Come forth, anointing of Jesus!" Come forth, anointing of the prophet! Come forth, prophetic insight and revelation! Come forth, opening of the Scriptures! Come forth! Come forth! Come forth!

And signs and wonders are going to begin to take place on the [school] campuses of Iowa --- at the high schools and junior high schools and the college campuses. The LORD says, "I AM inviting them with a Spirit of revelation and the miraculous signs and wonders. The signs and wonders will get their attention. The veil will lift, and I will bring revelation to them. And what you could not do in decades [on your own], I AM going to do in a day."

The LORD says, "It'll be even upon those who are bound by tradition, lifelessness, and religious spirits." The LORD says, "I AM coming to break that off of this state, and Iowa will be known as a wild place in the Spirit --- a radical place of revolutionary warriors, who move in radical zeal and boldness.

And right then, the full anointing shall break forth from the plains of Iowa. The fire of MY

Spirit is going to begin to burn through the dross, to colorize wounds and heal [the hurts]. It's going to heal, not only physical and emotional wounds, but the Body of Christ is going to be healed in [awesome] ways... There is coming a Spirit of healing, harmony, and unity that is going to be by the fire of MY Spirit, because I AM no longer going to be persuasive and speaking in ways that try to woo MY people into this, but," the LORD says, "I AM coming with a Holy Fire that is going to literally burn down walls that have separated and divided! And I AM coming with Holy Fire and passion [to] break into MY Church, even in places that they have not asked ME to. I'M going to do it anyway. I'M gonna move in and crash through walls and barriers. I'M going to lift fatigue and weariness off of MY people. MY leaders are going to be filled with fresh zeal, fresh fire, and fresh oil from MY Spirit." The LORD says, "As this Spirit of revelation begins to move in and among you, do not be surprised when I interrupt your gatherings with visions." I even see this. I see young children --- three, four, five, six years old, and upward --- moving into meetings where the adults are and saying, "I have just had a vision from God." And they will take over the meeting to share the vision that they have seen. "People will run for salvation, and deliverance will begin to take place as the children speak," the LORD says, "because I will give them revelation from heaven. And they will not argue with ME. They will say what I say, and they will say what I show them."

The LORD says, "This move of MY Spirit will not be built around the abilities of man. This move of MY Spirit will be built around ME and ME alone! This move of MY Spirit will require a [greater] level of humility." The LORD says, "I AM going to cause you to put your faces to the ground and cry out to ME in humility and lowliness of heart --- [to] know your need of God and revelation. You're going to have to acknowledge that you do not have the insight and the abilities to do this on your own." The LORD says, "You must be willing to acknowledge your failures and the plans of man that have fallen and [been] caused [or] inspired by demonic forces," the LORD says, "that have infiltrated through these things. But if you will humble yourself with a new spirit of humility and dependency, I AM going to react to that very quickly." The LORD says, "I AM going to move in quickly with a Spirit of grace and mercy and revelation. And I will show you how to turn years and decades around that the worms and the locusts have destroyed. I will come in MY great mercy and show you how to turn it around. And it will not take the same amount of time that it took for the enemy to do it [as it has been done in the past]. I will come and bring a Spirit of expediency upon it." The LORD says, "I will show you how to do it very quickly, but it will require great humility." The LORD says, "I say to you, 'You do not know how to do what I want you to do.' You do not have the understanding within yourself. You must lean upon ME! And you must look to MY Spirit to give you the plan. I say to you, 'I give you a promise.'" The LORD says, "If you will do this, I will come. I say to you, 'I will come!' I will rend the heavens. I will come to you! I will change [you]. And you will see that for which you cried... that for which you have wept. I say, 'Then you will call your sons and daughters from afar, and they will come.' I say [that] your words will begin to penetrate. And when you prophesy to the north, south, east, or west to give them up, I say, this time they will come. And I say that when I send you this time to the demonic strongholds of darkness, and you prophesy MY Word, they will fall. And you will break through," the LORD says.

Chuck Pierce Oct 27th 2003
Transcribed from Fifty State Tour

"The corn-belt states are going to rise up and learn a new way of releasing."

[Here] in Iowa, in the days ahead, you are about to be broken open in a way like never before.

There's one more verse I want to give you before Pastor Dutch comes. And it's out of Micah. It's a verse God gave me, for us, as we came here. Micah, chapter 4, verse 10. I believe it's a promise for us here. Verse 9 and 10… and I felt like it was very specific for Iowa.

"Now, why do you cry aloud? Is there no king in your midst? Has your counselor perished? For pains have seized you like a woman in labor. Be in pain and labor to bring forth, O daughter of Zion, like a woman in birth pangs. For now, you shall go forth from the city. You shall dwell in the field."

And the LORD also said this to me: "When you come to Iowa, you're going to pray for Iraq. And from Iowa, there will be a shift in Iraq that [will] begin to come as [you] stand and pray." HE said, "Once you get to the field, then from the field, go to Babylon and declare that [which] is still working in evil in the midst of that nation. There will be a supernatural shift. The Church will rise up. Harvest work will began to take place. Supplies will be released from Iowa, beginning in the field, [and] Babylon will start changing."

And the LORD would say to you, **"The birth pains will begin here in Iowa. I say, even the birth pains, for the course that this nation will take, will now begin. [However,] I say to you that you have a voice, but your voice is not resounding and being heard the way that I would have it heard. You have revelation, but you're not communicating your revelation. You have supply, but you're not [taking advantage of] your supply. So I would say [that] I AM starting the birth pains here in Iowa, for the future,"** saith the LORD. **"I say, begin to pray for the harvesters to arise from Iowa. And as you pray for the harvesters to arise, in four months, you will see the harvest in a new way. For I AM releasing a plan in this state [to] cause [this] harvest to be seen. And it will even be traced back into this state,"** saith the LORD. **"And I would say [that] from this state, Babylon will begin to change. For I will [make] a supernatural connection from the cornfields, the supply from this state that will change the course of the Church in Iraq,"** saith the LORD. **"I say, do not look at the confusion that is going on in that land. For, here in Iowa, you will have a supernatural authority to defeat Babylon in [the] days ahead."**

Dutch Sheets Oct 28th 2003
Transcribed from Fifty State tour

"What are YOU saying about Jericho to Iowa? And what are YOU saying about Ruth?" **We're going to see the fullness of [an] open heaven and all that [this] means. We're going to change the atmosphere [over] Iowa . This is [based on] faith, but it's also [based on] a Word from YOU, [LORD]. [Therefore,] we are laying hold of it, and we are going to see things change, [because of it]. Now help us today, LORD, as we speak about this, to say what needs to be said and move away from anything that is not from YOU. [Father,] help us to think with the mind of Christ and hear the [spoken] Word of the LORD. Thank YOU, LORD, for awakening [the] sleeping ones and replacing sleep with revelation. Thank YOU for doing it here as a first fruits for what is coming to the nation, because much of America is a sleep. LORD, let this be a true awakening. In fact, let a great awakening come to Iowa [and] to this [entire] nation. [Let it be] a great awakening... [Therefore, by faith,] we say [that] a great awakening is coming. Thank YOU, LORD. And what a great place... to let it begin here... Amen.**

Jericho is all about transitioning into the new. And so, if God is saying, " Jericho ," and [you need to] think " Jericho " when you think [about] Iowa right now, then HE is definitely saying, "New..." HE is saying, "Transition into the new." HE's saying, "There is a shift that [will be] taking place, and the wandering [will be] ending... The wilderness thing is ending, and it's time [for you] to move into [your] inheritance." And I think you can sense that. Jericho is all about new beginnings.

[And Chuck] talked about a Spirit of revelation [here in this state] that would touch the nation and the nations. That's very profound to me.

But God has HIS interesting way of doing things. And HE says, "Right out of Iowa, I'M going to bring forth revelation."

"There's something happening here that is a new beginning. It's a first fruits of what I'M gonna do elsewhere."

Because, if God is comparing this state to Jericho, [then] one of the things [that] HE [is] saying [to us] is that HE wants to begin bringing forth covenantal blessings from this state.

[Now, in all this,] what is God saying to Iowa ? HE's saying, "I'M going to cleanse [you]. I'M going to purge out [the] evil [from your midst].

I'M going to bring judgment to all that opposes ME; all of the idolatry, all of the carnality, all of the evil --- not people --- HE's not after people! HE's after demonic strongholds! HE's after the works of darkness! And HE's gonna say, "I'M gonna destroy it, I'M gonna bury it, and I'M gonna pull out that which is holy unto ME and raise up, as a covenantal offering unto ME, the holy and pure people of Iowa! I'M gonna set them apart unto ME and make them the first fruits, holy unto ME, blessed, MY treasure, MY harem!"

HE [hasn't] said that to any other state, by the way. I've not said that anywhere else we've been. Don't get the idea [that] we get this hot, fresh, wild teaching and then just go sprinkle it everywhere. This is special! This is very special! This very word should be treated as holy!

HE said, "I'M taking back MY earth!" Iowa ... "And I'M going to arouse, from here, the sleep. Revelation is gonna flow out of Iowa that awakens people in the nation and the nations of the earth. It's MY covenantal heartland."

What's HE saying to you, Iowa ? You better think about this one. Jubilee --- the Christ --- liberty --- freedom --- restoration --- [the] oppressed goin' free --- [the] broken-hearted --- healed --- restoration of the Land --- curses broken --- bridal intimacy --- separation unto HIM --- harem --- Iowa...

I think, by calling this place "Jubilee", HE was saying, "This city of sevens, you are giving to ME, is all about covenant and seven-ing yourselves, one to another. So you're gonna give ME the spoils, but I'M gonna give you Jubilee and all the [rest of the] Land. You have sevened yourself to ME. You entered into an oath when you gave ME the inheritance, the spoils, that which was [already] MINE; you sevened yourself with an oath and gave ME the offering."

And now HE's saying, "I'M gonna seven MYSELF to you, and I'M promising you Jubilee. I'M promising you to give you this Land [Israel]. I'M promising you that I'M freeing you once and for all from your slavery and oppression. And I'M going to give you this Land [of Israel] once and for all; it belongs to you.

I just heard the LORD say, "It's Jericho where you're going."

Now, in keeping with this Jubilee thing, in this type of Christ, what a lot of people don't think about --- they just don't realize --- [that] Boaz was born from Rahab. Rahab [a prostitute from Jericho] was taken by a man in Israel , married into the Abrahamic line --- the Covenantal family

--- she married Salmon. [Then] Salmon and Rahab had Boaz.

So, here we go again. HE's pulling [out] the redeemer kinsman, [the one] who would buy back the Land or take one who was widowed and marry her, [in order to] bring forth offspring. The whole picture of the redeemer kinsman, which was a picture of Christ, came out of Rahab, in Jericho.

#5) So now, we're [up] to Ruth! 'Cause the book of Ruth was borne out of Jericho ! So I" say to the LORD, "Alright, help me with this prophet who's given me this assignment, Jericho and Ruth; what's the connection?" I never thought about it before, so I started studyin'. EARLY, this morning, I started studyin'!... NOT sleeping in! And it finally hits, and I go, "DUH!... Boaz from Rahab!..." So the whole story of Ruth, then, springs out of Jericho.

And now we're to this thing that he kept saying, "I see the bread thing." Now, [speaking to Chuck Pierce,] you may have to come up and tell me what you were seeing. But he kept saying, the four corners, and like Ruth gleaned from the corners of the field, something happening in the four corners of Iowa, moving to the center. And then he starts prophesying about feeding the nation, the bread of heaven, the revelation, and

I'm sayin', "Alright, LORD, put this together for me."

HE's saying, "You are gleaners. You are going to bring forth from the earth in the same way as Ruth and Boaz. It wasn't just about feeding bread to people, it's about picturing something else. It's all about the Bread of Heaven. [God is saying,] "I'm trying to paint a picture in this book that I'M bringing forth the Bread of Life, from the field of Boaz, in Bethlehem." And HE's saying, "From Iowa, I want to feed the nations of the earth, and not just physical food, but the Bread of Heaven! I want you to glean, from the four corners --- and then the center --- of this state, the wealth of Heaven! And I want you to export it to the nations, so I can awaken a people! So I can bring forth MY Covenant! So I can bring Jubilee into the Land and let the oppressed go free --- to set at liberty the broken and the bruised. I want to restore! I want to let the captives go free! I want somebody to run throughout the land and say, 'FREEDOM! LIBERTY!'" Ring the bell of freedom.

You know what? I think Jericho, the most fortified city, becomes a place of provision. **HE's saying, "Out of the greatest of your enemies, I'M gonna bring your Provision. Out of your greatest enemies, I'M gonna bring forth something of**

Christ. I'll transform everything [your enemy] tries to oppress you, destroy you, and keep you from [receiving] your inheritance. I'll show you MY Seed in it. And I'll show you how I want to redeem it and bring forth the riches of your inheritance."

I'm saying to you, "You've come to the fullness of time." You have come to a fullness of time. Do not miss this! There is a window of opportunity [which] HE has opened for you. Do not miss this Iowa . You have come to a fullness of time.

You must go all the way now! You must push! You have come to transition. You must spring to birth. You must! There are enough of you to do this. You do not need a majority. You just need what you have. There are plenty of you that know how to do this. Go to the four corners and worship. Go to the four corners and decree. Go to the four corners and point to the middle of this state.

God said to me, when I walked into my hotel room yesterday, **"I AM about to uncover the darkness. I AM about to expose the darkness over this state, the deceit, and the sin. HE will expose these strongholds that Chuck was talkin' about when I walked in [here] this morning. [Chuck was talking about] something in these cornfields of Iowa ; there is evil there. But I'm tellin' ya, just like there are strongholds over this state --- and** they're over all the states, God is going to show you how to deal with that quickly, because you are in a fullness of time. [God says,] "Your sons and daughters are comin' home. The prodigals are comin' home. I'M gonna take care of everything." And HE [will] dislodge things, 'cause it's a fullness of time. I'm tellin' ya it is.

Expect governmental changes in Iowa ! And I mean natural government. And I don't even know enough about it to know what needs to happen, but I'm tellin' you right now, that's what I just heard in my spirit; expect governmental changes! In fact, expect some radical things that nobody [has] anticipated.

What is [God] saying to Iowa about that? HE's saying, "It's the fullness of time, and it's time for you to come into [your] fullness." It's a fullness of time, but it's time to [also] come into fullness. And as you come into fullness, you're coming into a fullness of anointing. You know, you can preach. You can minister. You can do something, and you can do it at a certain level. Then, [as you exercise the anointing given to you,] God moves you to a higher level of anointing. [Once HE has accomplished this in you, then] you [will] do the same thing, say the same thing, and pray the same thing, and it [will] bear more fruit and accomplish ten times as much. [And, all the

while,] you didn't change a thing. You didn't change any of your delivery [or] pray any differently.

So, what **HE's saying to you is, "Come up higher! Come into the fullness of the Christ anointing. Be an apostolic state! Be a prophetic state! Come fully into your prophetic anointing! Go into the heavenlies and break through! Prepare the way for others! Go to another [higher] level of the prophetic mantle [and] enter into the fullness of it. Move into the fullness of evangelism --- into the fullness of pastoring and teaching. Move into the fullness of the Christ anointing.**

And I say to Iowa, come into the fullness of your reward. Glean from the four corners all that God has for you. Go and take back the spoils that HE has promised you. Go to the four corners of the state and say, "This is now separated unto God. It is holy unto HIM. This state is part of HIS harem. It's a part of HIS first fruits offering. We swear an oath to HIM that all of Iowa belongs to HIM. It's HIS inheritance. No one else can have any of it. We've kicked all the Achans out of this state." We say that no one will steal HIS inheritance in Iowa. No one can have HIS inheritance. Jericho belongs to HIM. Iowa belongs to HIM. The state belongs to HIM.

Chuck Pierce October 28th 2003
Transcribed from the Fifty state Tour

I could look down and see the state and various things goin' on within the state. Around Des Moines, there's this big circle of darkness. I don't know how to say it nicely, and yet, know that you're encircled by darkness. There is an occult force that has access into these cornfields.

Now, Iowa, get ready; the prophetic anointing's gonna get dropped on you. It has to get dropped on ya, because there's a lot of occult spirits in your midst. And that tells me [that] you're a supernatural state and a supernatural people. You gotta become [a] supernatural people. There's a veil over the northeast [portion of Iowa]. God wants that veil lifted, because that means [that] there's great revelation [that] HE wants to bring into the northeast [corner of the state]. But there's a veil holding it. Something [is either] in the atmosphere or in the land, whether it be bloodshed or covenant breaking. There [are] four things to look at: bloodshed, covenant-breaking, idolatry, or immorality. [If one or more of these things] has occurred, [then it] has affected the land. And it's caused the land to be veiled. Therefore, God's purposes are not breaking forth. And, for God to show us that veil, that means HE wants us to break [through with] HIS purposes and rip the veil off.

Now, that veil, [in] some way, is linked to a darker system that is around Des Moines. So there's something originating [from] there that's linked into this city as a networking hub. And you're [probably thinking], "How in the world is he saying this?" Well, we live in the heavenlies. I don't live down here on earth... I don't... I want to walk in the earth realm, but I want to live in the heavenlies. I wanna see from the heavenlies. I wanna war from the heavenlies.

The heavens have already opened up and started declaring over Iowa what needs to be --- day by day, declaring what needs to be declared over Iowa. But some way or another, we [need] to have people down here [who will] come into agreement with it and start echoing it back. And then you'll start seeing this manifestation of what the heavens are declaring. That's the Lord's Prayer.

And in these cornfield states, I feel like God's putting an anointing on you to set a course that no one else can set for our nation. You're farmers... You're called to get up early... It's part of the inheritance of these states. And so, you have the authority to come into agreement with God and set a whole course for this nation.

[There's] a big circle of death around Des Moines. [And there's] so much death down in the southeast corner [of the state] that it's causing weeping to occur. God says, "You weep over that [which] you've allowed into the corner of this state." And there's a darkness up in the northeast corner that's causing a connection of this [circle around Des Moines] to stay in place.

Cindy Jacobs   Jan. 8th 2006
Denton, Texas

Oh, listen Iowa. Iowa listen. God says to you, I am coming for that corn state. The Lord says get ready for the move of God there in Iowa. I am coming to begin to release a new wine anointing upon that state. And the Lord says, corn and cattle, look to the cattle industry in Texas. I'm going to begin to move, things are going to get shaken. But God says if you will pray, I will save you from the plague and the mad cow disease, even up into Canada and into Mexico. God says there is going to be new breeds of cattle. I am going to cause hybrid breeds. God is going to bring new breeds that are resistant to mad cow disease.

Greg Crawford   June 10th 2006
"A New Season in Iowa"

There is a new sound that is coming, like as they blew the trumpet in Lev. 25 and released Jubilee upon the land. The trumpet is going to sound in Des Moines, there is going to be something released in the land in the state of Iowa. There is going to be a liberty and freedom that is coming that has never been before. Because this is the time and season. There is a sound even the dry bones are going to live again. There was a voice, there was a calling out, there was coming forth, with something that was spoken. There was a sound that caused them to come together. There is a sound that is going to be released, that is going to cause a coming together in Des Moines. There is a coming together. There is a sound that is coming, that is going to release the sound of a trumpet in the land, and it is going to release freedom from captivity. There is going to be a turning, a great turning, even in Cedar Rapids. Apostles and prophets are coming forth. They are going to be restored. Some are going to be restored in that season, in that moment. They are coming. This is a new season upon the Church. It is upon us. The seventh month and the tenth day a trumpet is sounding from heaven. The sound will be released in five days. It will take five days to process the word of the Lord. It will be released in Des Moines and it will go through the state. It is the fire that others have seen in times past going across the prairie. There is a fire coming. It is coming down off the mount. The completeness of all things.

We decree God tonight a sound from heaven. A sound, a rallying call. A trumpet. That you would put in the hearts of leaders that they would rally as one. As one voice in this hour and season. With one purpose of heart you are going to divide the two kingdoms .

The idols are coming down. The four are coming down. The four things are going to be revealed. A prophet is going to speak to it. A new season is upon you. The Josephs are coming out of the cave. They are coming out. The Davids are coming out. It is a season of deliverance in the land. The deliverance is coming. The deliverance of imprisonment. They are coming out of the cave and into the promotion. They are going to speak to kings. They are going to stand before great and mighty leaders. You must decree. This is the year of sevens. It is a joining of Davids and Josephs. A joining of the Ephraims and the Judahs. Two sticks becoming one. Two covenants being one. Two offices being one. A release of all things. Indebtedness off the Church. Release of bondage off the Church. The restoration of things, of families and lives.

W.A.R. Conference Bob Newton Jan 20th 2007

For I have marked the third month of this year, saith the Lord. And I shall set an angel on the four corners of this state. When their feet set upon the four corners of the state, their hands shall move back the veil that has covered this place, saith the Lord. There shall be a seven-months-opening of the heavens and when this happens, it shall be as a lamp in the middle of this state. It shall be as a lighthouse; that will shoot a beam to the north, and the south, and the east and the west. And when that fire, when that lamp, touches the west it shall set the fields on fire. And when it touches the east it shall rise as a flood for there shall be a move of My Spirit, saith the Lord. When My angels set their feet on the corners of this state, I have marked the third month of this year, there shall be seven months of outpouring for the windows of heaven shall be open upon this place, saith the Lord.

Iowa Alliance for Reformation Meeting 02/27/07

Fire is coming to the campuses of Iowa.

The shift will come when the trumpet of gathering has ended over the state. At this time, all the brethren who have been called will come. Angels will be seen in the night sky over Iowa and they will resemble fireflies. They will be fiery ones lighting up the vials and releasing a residue in the night. There is famine in the land and it is a famine of manna. Intercessors are to be face down while famine is in the land. There must be repentance for the structures men have created and the programs they have made. They have nothing. They are whitewashed tombs. You do not see what I see. A season of travail will cost you in tears and mourning. Do you not see what grieves my heart? The angels will carry vials of blessings to make it through the temporary season.

Word for Iowa from Apostle Greg Crawford - June 5, 2008

Even as my son David could not build my house

because he fell into sin, it was the spirit of Saul that influenced him. All he could do was prepare for the building but he could not build what I wanted to build. And many leaders are in that same place. It is not because they have fallen into sin, it is because they allow the spirit of Saul to influence them. So they have only been able to prepare for the building and have not been able to build.

But I say I am about to raise the sons and daughters and the offspring, and they shall build my house. And even as you have been fighting and in this war with Saul for seven years, I say I shall begin to build My house for seven years in this state, like My son David did and My son Solomon did. And My house shall be built according to My pattern. There shall be a building of My house in this state over the next seven years. And the splendor of it shall begin to be increased, and the glory of it shall be known.

I say at the end of the seven years men and women will come to this state to seek My presence and My glory. And My wisdom shall begin to flow into their hearts. I say do not just begin to build for the moment that you are living in, but build for the future of what you shall become. I say I'm building something in this hour, and I am laying the foundations once again in My house. The cornerstone has been laid and the foundations to homes are now being set. And I am about to raise something of My presence within your very lives, and you have to fit into what I am building in this hour.

For I say the spirit of Saul has been put off. You have put it off of your lives. You have not allowed it to influence you. Some have allowed it to come and have walked away, and fallen back. But I say this is the hour, for much preparation has occurred in my leaders. They have prepared much, but cannot build anything. They have put aside, but cannot see the pattern.

I say I am about to release a pattern into My sons and daughters and they shall build for My glory and not for their own glory. They shall build for My presence and not for My blessing to be upon their life. They shall build what I have prepared and laid in place. They shall understand how to fit it skillfully and fit it lively into place and lovingly into place. And they shall understand the pattern, not seeing the finish. They shall know they are building what I have declared. They shall understand there is a pattern that has come down.

And I say for seven years, for seven years, mark for seven years My splendor shall be becoming more and more evident and My glory shall become more and more evident. Even like Solomon built, you shall build visitation, a habitation, a dwelling place for My presence to come. And this state shall feel it. This nation shall know it. I say what I am building many will run into, many will come, many will come, many will come, many will come, and the words of My prophets shall be fulfilled. And this state will double in population, it will triple in population. For they will come to see My glory, to see My glory, see My glory!

From Cindy Jacobs   "Arise Iowa"
Morning Session Prophecy

"Iowa is called to change world affairs."
This is a tipping point time, where God wants to throw this state into a massive move of God. You're just on the verge. I could almost say the birth pangs of revival.

I was thinking about these roots of reformation, and what I feel is this place is where God wants to light a great fire of reformation.

He said, "They're an Issachar state,"
The state is going to grow and double in population in the next few years, because God is going to bring in… there's going to be new companies moving in, there's going to be whole new cities built. The Lord shows me that the flight that has happened in Iowa will be reversed. And it's not going to hurt the farming. The Lord has shown me that He's going to balance this all out, because He loves the land.

For the Lord says, "Iowa shall be a state of visitation… Iowa shall come into a state of visitation," says the Lord. Not only have you been visited by the politicians and the politicos, but the Lord says, "You're going to be visited by Me," says the Lord. "You're going to be visited by My power," says God. "Iowa will be a state of miracles," says God. The Lord says, "I am going to pour out signs and wonders upon this state," says the Holy Spirit. "I am going to do wonders, not only are there going to be physical manifestations and bodies, but I'm going to do wonders in the heavens, creative miracles. I am the God of creation, and I never stopped being the God of creation," says the Lord. So you're going to see, just as in Almalonga, Guatemala, there were giant vegetables, "I am going to begin to kiss and bless the land here like the Garden of Eden," and the Lord says, "I am going to bless the produce." And God says, "Award winning vegetables." God says, "I am going to begin to give the increase, the curse is being broken off the land," says God. And God says, " I am going to release," and I don't know what's in the very north, but the Lord says, "There's a fire in the north, there's fire in the north. I am going to pour down from the north," says the Lord, "and I am going to visit the frozen places with my fire," says the Lord, "and I am going to begin to heat up this state," says God, "and I am going to visit the Lutheran churches, look and see, for the fire of reformation will once again burn in My German people," says the Lord. And the Lord says, "The fire of the Holy Spirit is going to come, for I am going to light up this place with My northern lights. I am going to release My glory," says God.

"And I am going to cause 24/7 prayer houses to spring up. Look to the University of Iowa," says God, "for I am coming for a great visitation. I am going to shift it from the left to the right. For I am coming in a major shift, for this is a tipping point time," says God, "I am getting ready to tip it", says the Lord. And the

Lord says, "And not only that, you've only seen the tip of the iceberg of what I am getting ready to do because," the Lord says, "come let us go onto the mountain of the Lord. I am getting ready to release the nations to flow into Iowa." God says, "New airports… there will be airport expansions. You're going to see new things," says God. I'm going to put this on the tape, "And the population will double," God says. "Get ready Iowans, buy land, buy land, buy land, buy land before the prices shoot up! Buy in Iowa!" says God, "Buy in those places that everybody moved out of, because I'm getting ready to move in!" says the Lord. Amen.

This state is a command post for understanding prophetic intelligence that will change the nations of the earth.

You'll actually be bi-vocational. You're going to see more and more pastors that God is going to anoint them. They'll have a marketplace anointing, as well as an anointing to preach. And you're going to see both of this happening. But one of the other words that God gave us for '08 is that you're going to be able to work less and make more.

There's a generation of young seers arising that are like nothing we have ever known. And the children and the youth of this state are seers… This young guy got up on the table in the cafeteria, Lou told me this story, and just started preaching and preaching, and a teacher pulled him off the lunch table. And a girl got up in his place and she started preaching and preaching, and they called the principal. And he pulled her down, and then another kid jumped up, and it's like they couldn't stop them. But you know what stopped the move of God, was the parents.

    Iowa is a Daniel and a Joseph state, which is under the purview of Issachar. And I just mean that I feel that they're all connected together. So Daniels and Josephs, you're' governmental, but you have a Joseph anointing. So what you're going to see one day, and I've not prophesied this in any other state, is that there will be a national poll taken, and the number of entrepreneurs, and new business startups that come from Iowa will exceed all the other states.

    You are Cyruses, and you have just known that there was oil under the ground. But the Lord shows me that there's some of you that God is going to show you where that oil is. So Father, we call forth the oil that has been…oh, no, it's gasoline…the petroleum, that's what it is…petroleum resources that are under the ground. Something to do with the northeastern part of this state. Lord, in the name of Jesus, we call in these reserves that are reserved until the end-times.

Chapter 4

The Four Anointings for Iowa

This is a Revelation type word the Lord gave me concerning the state of Iowa. This is in transcript form as it was preached.

We're going to start in Philippians and I'm going to read about two pieces of scripture tonight and talk about four books. ***Phil. 3:17*** –is where I'm going to start.

Philippians 3:17, -"*brethren, be followers together of me, and mark them which walk so as ye have us for an example*". Vs. 18 "*for many walk, of whom I have told you often, and now tell you even weeping, that they are the enemies of the cross of Christ.* Vs.19. '*whose end is destruction, whose God is their belly, and whose glory is in their shame, who mind earthly things*. Vs. 20. '***For <u>our conversation</u> is in heaven; from whence also we look for the saviour, the Lord***

Jesus Christ; Vs. 21- '***who shall change our vile body, that it may be fashioned like unto his glorious body, according to the working where by he is able even to subdue all things unto himself'.***

The word conversation means = the administration of civil affairs or common wealth. It does not mean we're having a dialogue or talking. It means that we are administrating something, the civil affairs. It even means the form of government and laws by which something has been administrated. So you see, we last Saturday night discussed that our identification is being talked about in heaven. There's a conversation going on about you right now in heaven.

And we see that Mary, in *Luke 1:26* -an angel came to give her identity, so that she could accomplish something, which was birthing the king together. And that the **king** and **kingdom** is setting inside the Church right now and God is trying to give the Church an **identity.** Now, you see where God is at tonight, it's how do you release this identity, or what identity is coming to us? There is a conversation going on in heaven, and here is part of the conversation, it's about the administration of God's Kingdom in your life. That is part of this conversation that's going on. It even means, to talk about the commonwealth of citizens. So, sitting tonight there is an administration of our life in heaven being discussed, and the earth is about to get some angelic visitations to release that identity into us. That's what is coming! And so, the question is what is stopping the administration of the Kingdom in our life?

It's right in the same verse here in ***Phil.3: 18-19.*** People are minding earthly things. Considering earthly things more than God. They are putting everything before him -conversations, affections, what we spend our finances on. It even talks about what we feed our belly, and other things. It actually means to not have a fasted lifestyle. It's talking about the things that we do, to avoid doing what God asked us to do. We're supposed to be living a fasted life style. Jesus said, 'some of these don't come out, but by prayer and fasting. We will pray, but we won't fast.

Now, I'm not going to talk about fasting tonight. But he says, 'they're able to subdue things, that when all this starts getting into order, things start getting subdued. The word **subdued means**—'to be put subject to, or 'under subject to'. But it also comes down to this, 'a military fashion under the command of a leader'. So, when we start becoming militant about who we are, and what we can accomplish...

Tonight, during intercession, God was giving me this, releasing this strategy over this state, and He was even giving cities to go to. He was giving me assignments cause we want to move this state. We want to see something happen. God does not want us sitting here tonight--doing a ministry thing, that we gather, we sing a few sing-along songs and we don't accomplish any thing. I want my conversation to count. I want to know what is being spoken in heaven, and I tell you, what's being spoken in heaven, God's talking about strategy right now. He's talking about how the Church is going to govern the affairs of men and change society. That's what He's talking about! Let's go to the second scripture.

Four Horns and Four Carpenters

Zechariah 1:18 "Then I lifted up mine eyes and saw and behold four horns. And I said unto the angel that talked with me, what be these? And he answered me, these are the horns, which have scattered Judah, Israel, and Jerusalem, and the Lord showed me four carpenters, vs. 21, then said I, what come these to do? And he spoke, saying, these are the horns which scattered Judah, so that no man did lift up his head; but these are come to fray them, to cast out the horns of the Gentiles, which lift up their horn over the land of Judah to scatter it."

It talks about four horns, four carpenters. Communism=a religiousless society. A society with absolutely no religion. The second horn is radical

Islam = which brings a false religion into society and government. The third one is Hinduism = which is idolatry, Babylon, and fourth horn= terrorism, which is a society, based on fear. And those four horns are touching Judah, Jerusalem, and Israel.

Judah means = praise. Praise; it doesn't mean praised with a 'd' on the end. Yes, it isn't talking about a current action. It's talking about a past action that has happened. That means, if you start looking at it, here's the reality, what has been praised, or what has gone up in praise throughout the earth has one of these four things attacking it tonight. The Church is under attack by one of these four things, no matter where you live on earth.

But he says, "I'm sending four carpenters, four master builders, four engravers, four plowers who will plow something. He says, "I'm sending them and they're going to fray them, and they're going to cast out, and scatter them. What does fray mean? 'To terrify, to tremble, to quake'. These four carpenters are going to cause fear in those four horns: communism, radical Islam, Hinduism, and terrorism.

There was a prophetic word over the state of Iowa from Dutch Sheets and Chuck Pierce, that we would touch Iraq, and that Babylon would be touched through Iowa. The prophetic word said that they would be cast out, or thrown down. But it also means to praise and give thanks. It tells you the action of the casting down and how it's going to occur. Now with all that, that's the introduction.

Four horns, four carpenters. –Kim Clement released this word this week, and here's what it says, "My Kingdom is about to appear, yes, it's about to appear, as it appeared to Daniel, Joseph, Isaiah, and Enoch. He talks about four appearings of a kingdom coming, and he says, Four great anointings are coming into the earth. Then he goes on and he says, ' God says, you have every Babylonian nation staring once again, but they are not staring at Democrats or Republicans, they are staring for the spirit of Daniel! They are afraid that a David might arise. They are afraid that someone might come forth from the prison.

Like Joseph, and arise. They are looking for the signs of Davids emerging, and are looking for the signs of Isaiahs and of Daniel, Shadrach, Meshach, and Abednego emerging. And once again Babylon will be invaded by the power of the living God.

Four Kingdom Anointings For Iowa

Now, that's pretty intense. The reason I've pulled this section out of all this, is the fact that he talks about these four anointings twice. Now I have enough sense to know that if God is talking about something twice, you had better pay attention. With that, here's what the Lord started speaking to me. So we should all know the story of Joseph and Daniel. We probably won't know the story of Enoch, cause there are only 5 verses, but there is actually a whole book of Enoch- of Enoch and the Watchers, and all of these other books that you can read about Enoch, and we should all know this. Here's what the Lord spoke to me.

There are four dynamics of the Kingdom that are about to be released, and those four dynamics are coming to this state. God is about to release four apostolic voices in this state. These four voices are going to align with heaven. It is the alignment with the four beasts around the throne coming to the earth.

There is the alignment of what is already in heaven coming down to the earth. There is an alignment of anointing, and visitation in the throne room that is coming through these four anointings. These four men's lives are the identity that is coming into the Church. These four lives are the identity of the next generation that will capture this. This anointing is coming to release, to release a Kingdom. Anointing is a divine enablement of God to release the Kingdom of God.

There is an enablement of God that came into

Mary's life to confront the fact that she conceived by the Holy Spirit and had a visitation with her identity.

God is about to visit the anointing of these four types of kingdoms that are coming to bring an identity into The Church that is lacking right now in this hour, because all four of these are a confrontational identity.

These four men even thought Isaiah was a prophet. We concluded three were apostolic and one was prophetic, but I believe even Isaiah was apostolic in nature, because he established some foundations that were lacking. So, there's a four-fold apostolic anointing coming into The Church in this next year.

That is what we are about to participate in. God is about to bring in that anointing so we will identify with it and release the Kingdom through it. The alignment of the four beasts around the throne with the multifaceted eyes, they have an assignment around the throne, and this anointing that's coming into the earth has an assignment in the earth.

Builder Anointings

These four anointings are builder anointings. The Lord spoke to me, that *Jeremiah 1:10* is concluding at the end of this year, that there will not be any more tearing down, there will be a building up now. He's loosing a four-fold anointing to do it- to build and establish and bring reformation, transformation and every kind of 'ation' there is. It is coming to the earth. It is coming finally. So, this identification: Here's what the names mean:

Joseph means = God has added.

Daniel means = judged of God.

Isaiah means -salvation of Jehovah, -which we're going to see.

Enoch means = dedicated.

These are the identity that God is trying to bring into The Church.

God has added. Not man. Not a Saul structure, but a Davidical structure. God has added. Daniel, the judge of God, we're going to see the justice of God finally start to unleash this year. What was the year of jubilee that we talked about in *Leviticus 25*? It talks about jubilee.

What is the year of jubilee about? Seeing justice come for those that are impoverished. It was about justice.

Isaiah = salvation of Jehovah.

We understand that we are carriers of salvation, of reformation to release deliverance. And Enoch dedicated. It will take a greater dedication than The

Church has seen.

Passion and intimacy will go to a new level next year. It will come to a higher realization that it is a necessity to survive what we are about to do. In that music CD that Josh (Crawford) is mixing to record that song that they have done, Josh told me that these four names were spoken. We spoke these four names out in advance of this. All four of these people started their entire ministry at 17-18 years old. They were all young. They were all called out at a young age to do something that was radical for the Kingdom to shift something. They all carried an anointing, and here's a reality, when you recognize the anointing on your life, you will settle your identity.

The anointing is coming this year to settle the identity of the Church once and for all, and His people, so that confidence and boldness will come, and we will accomplish the birthing forth of the Kingdom, finally. We have only been forerunning that which is about to be. It's intense, isn't it? Let's talk about each of these four.

Enoch -saw the Kingdom as it is.

There are 5-7 scriptures about Enoch.**Heb.11: 5, Gen. 5:22, Jude 1:14.** What do we know about Enoch? That he pleased God. He's in the hallmark of faith. He was a person of great faith. Enoch was the first that was to die, but did not die-after Adam. Yes, isn't that interesting?

Enoch is about living in the eternity of God, and not experiencing death. Enoch is about being the friend of God. This is where you are going with your identity next year. You're going to be the friend of God in the way you've never been. You're going to learn to live in the eternity of God, and not fear death or fear the things that come. Enoch had visitations from God. In the book of Enoch, here's what he actually says, he says, "the Lord opened his eyes to see who he was in heaven". That's how he got his identity. There was an opening of his spiritual eyes to see his identity that he had never seen. But he also saw it in ***Jude 1:14,*** somebody coming with 10,000 that destroyed Babylon. The very warning of Zechariah, is that not something? So, here's what **Enoch is also about, seeing the Kingdom as it is.** Here's the anointing that was on his life, the anointing that is coming to The Church. **An anointing to enter the revelatory realm.** Because Enoch went up and down, up and down, up and down with God, and God spoke to him and said to confront these things on the earth, and he had watcher angels that he was in charge of. You've got to read the book of Enoch. **Enoch is about the translation of humanity.** He was translated from a regular man to a heavenly basis with God. What was he building? He was a carpenter before. **He was building a relationship with God**. Here's what else it's about. It's about **living in miracles that supersede time and space**. Living in a spirit realm that supersedes the natural. That's where he lived, where he moved. God spoke to him. What did God say? Back in Genesis **"*and he was no more.*"** What does that mean? God took him, because he was spending so much time with God, He decided no sense in you going back home (to earth). You've been going back, going back and going back, and they won't listen, so guess what we're going to do? We're going to flood the earth. That's why it happened, they wouldn't listen to Enoch. He says, I'm going to take care of this, and we're going to start something new, and I'm going to get rid of all those watchers and all that stuff going on. So, you see **Enoch was anointed to go to the revelatory realm**. It's about the translation of humanity. It's about building a relationship with God. It is about the Kingdom as it is.

Joseph —'the kingdom in the now.'

Joseph was a dreamer, ***Gen. 37;*** his dreams got him into trouble. His brothers forsook him. His family forsook him. We are in a generation that is experiencing this dream in their heart, forsaken by all.

He was sold into slavery. Put in prison. Not able to come out, but there was somewhere that he got his identity. Somewhere he connected and found out who he was, and he got out of where he was. That's what's coming next year. There is a multitude coming out of the prison where they have been, because they are about to get an identity from God, and I'll tell you where the identity is, it's sitting 'inside of them, right now! ***Psalm 105:16,*** says this**, "*more over he called for a famine upon the land: he broke the whole staff of bread."*** Who called for the famine? God did. I think we're in famine, somewhat in this land, and I think it's God's hand to get us on our knees. "He sent a man before them, even Joseph, who was sold for a servant:" **Vs. 18-19 "*Whose feet they hurt with fetters; he was laid in iron: Until the time that his word came.*"** The word of the Lord tried him." The word was sitting inside Joseph. **Sitting inside a lot of our young people is a dream and a word**. It's sitting inside of them, but God has to try you, if you're going to believe it or not.

But, boy! If you're going to believe it, guess what's going to happen? You're going to come out of your prison house, and you're going to really go and do something, because here's what he was anointed to do. **He is in the lineage of Issachar. There is an anointing coming into the Church to know the time and season of the land. This anointing is for**

the transformation of a nation. Enoch was about the translation of humanity to third heaven. This is about the transformation of a nation, and what is he building? **He was building a refuge for an entire nation**. You see inside of him was the promise of his destiny and his purpose and his identity, all wrapped into one. Everybody was telling him, it's like this, and it's like this, and it's like this, but the wisdom of God was birthed, as he worked out the process. We're going to see the wisdom of God come out of a generation that will supercede anything that we could ever imagine. It's coming forth!

Isaiah saw the Kingdom in the beginning.

Isaiah 22 He saw Jesus. He saw the government upon his shoulders. He saw a man that was deformed and beaten. The beginning of the Kingdom on the earth. He saw it! You know what he was anointed to do? **He was anointed to declare that Kingdom! No matter who opposed**, he declared.

There was **an anointing in his life to voice and be a spokesman and a trumpet in the earth**. You know what it is about? **The reformation of mindset and belief.** You see, it's progressive. God is about to reform us in what we believe. There's an anointing coming to reform. Think about it! Because the Lord spoke, four apostles in this state with this anointing are coming. This thing is coming into this state. There is a fourfold anointing that's coming. It will be. The Lord spoke to me earlier, it will be the fullness of the gospel, it will be the fullness. It will not be lacking in any part. It will take a dimension of one of the gospels. This fourfold anointing will lead into each gospel. It will be the fullness of what we've been looking for. *Isaiah 6:1.* He got his identity and his assignment all at the same time. This thing is going to accelerate, and that has been the word of the Lord by the prophets in the last two weeks. That acceleration is coming into the Body for 2007, not only are you going to get identity, you're going to get assignment, you're going to get purpose, you're going to get under-standing. You're going to get the whole thing, all at once. It's coming, this is all coming, I'm telling you!

His identity came as he saw the throne. **He identified with what he had to build on earth.** This brought him to Jesus, the master builder, to get the pattern for the earth. In *Isaiah 2,* we had the whole conference on it, and what did He say we have to do? Establish the mountain, to build the house. What was he building? **What Isaiah was building, what is coming, this anointing is coming, is to finally establish to build God's house.** We forerunnered it this year. We are catching bits of these things.

Daniel; he sees the Kingdom in the future.

God says, seal the book, Daniel, for a generation. The word **'seal' doesn't mean you can't have access, it means that some people just can't look in, like the devil.** What it means, well it doesn't mean you'll never know. It means that there are some people that won't be able to look at it. You see, when **Jesus** took the book and opened it and broke the seal, **He** was able to peer in and look at it. This is the book that we will look in and peer and see what Daniel saw, right now, and these four things coming into the Church. And he saw the horns, where Mike (Lauer) started out tonight in intercession. In *Daniel 7*, he says, I see four horns, but I see a horn rising up. We'd better go back and read that, hadn't we?

He saw the Kingdom in the future. He was a judge who defended the fatherless and the widows. He interpreted dreams. He was known for wisdom and leadership, and character and integrity. You know what he was anointed for? **He was anointed as a spokesman for God's interpretation.** Not man's. Not denominations. Not organizations, but God's interpretation and what He was about. It was about transitioning a nation. Transforming, transitioning, moving, shifting, and what was He building? **I'll tell you what He was building! A reverence for God.** There was a Godly reverence that came out of his life and ministry, and the anointing he carried.

Daniel got his identification in ***Daniel 1:8***. – Daniel purposed in his heart, that he would not defile himself with the portion of the king's meat or wine, which the king drank. Therefore, he requested of the prince of the eunuchs that he might not defile himself. It's where we started in ***Philippians 3:18-19.*** Here's where he got his identity. His identity was already in his heart. And by making a decision, 'I will separate myself from the world', he gained his identity. He realized there was an anointing on his life, of separation, and he walked it out, because he knew that was his identity.

1. Four anointings releasing Four Kingdom Dynamics

That separation is coming into this next year into The Church and the generation that's coming up,

They will have an ability to separate themselves from worldly things, and live a life that many would desire to have. They will be able to live a life so that others will see a difference- that there is a God to follow It's coming into your life, young people, and you better grab it! Every identity will be proven. Identity is who and what you have aligned your affections with. Now here's the deal! God only promotes proven identity! The promotion of The Kingdom is the promotion. In all of these men's lives, The Kingdom was promotion. These four anointings are coming to The Church next year to release four dynamics of the kingdom. Better grab it!

Four men in the fiery furnace. They always think of Shadrach, Meshach, Abednego, but Jesus was in there as well. There are four men. There were four builders inside to build a nation, and they're in the fire, and the Son of God descended, that is coming to the Church this next year. That is coming into the Church, God is about to try with fire our identity. But if we will hold fast to what we know to be true, He will be in the midst of the accomplishments

You have to arise! You can't just sit around and think this is going to come on you. This is what's coming, but God's expecting you to rise up and take hold of it. We're all the friends of God, but God's going to take things deeper into our lives.

Four anointings are coming to release four dynamics of The Kingdom, and they are coming into this state. I saw them tonight in intercession descending. There are Kingdom dynamics happening. Seriously, this is the word of the Lord. This is for the next year, where the Church is going. There are some other things coming too, but this is a huge part of this. Here we sit tonight, we've gathered. You see, this isn't just to hear some little message thing. There are too many souls at stake for us to play with this. People are depending on us to get our self together. We can't wait for them to get together. They're waiting on us. We've got the wrong identity. But what you can do is make a commitment before God and these witnesses that you're after a new identity. Then we know, and God knows, that you've made a commitment to chase after this thing.

So, tonight, I'm going to end with this, if that is you, and you say, 'I want a new identity. I want you to stand up. I don't want you to stand because others are standing. This is serious! This is very serious! You stand, because God is convicting you and you know that you need that identity to become who you need to be. He's coming.

Father, tonight, I ask that you, Holy Spirit, see everything that is going on in this room. Every word that has been spoken I ask, God, that you look into the hearts of all of us sitting here, that you would try us. Try the word that is in us, like you did Joseph. God, that you would try us to see that we have integrity like Enoch, and God, that you would see that we would reverence you and live a Godly life, like Daniel. Father, take us into the place where we could be spokesmen like Isaiah and declare the word of the

Lord, and even as we're being martyred and sawed in half like a log. Prophesy to those doing it, the word of the Lord for the nation. We've got to have an eternal perspective on things, oh God! Our identity has to be eternal. Not temporal, and not earthly. God, I ask for release of identity of your people tonight, as we engage into this next year, we come into it God, I believe on January first, that night and the New Year begins, that you are going to release an identity and an assignment upon every person. You are bringing us into a new place. Father tonight, deal with our hearts in the days to come that we will be prepared to receive this. We determine tonight, even as we get up out of our chair, that we will arise and come after this.

Father, I thank you for every person that came here tonight, may they carry your anointing back into their churches as leaven and leaven this region oh, God! For reformation and change and awakening to come. God, I thank you for what you are doing in the youth in this city, right now, that there is something stirring and moving and changing in them. God, let it increase, let them know their identity even more. Father, I just thank you for everything that you have done in our midst. Work in our lives, Holy Spirit this week. Show us our assignment tomorrow of what we are to do and where we are to go.

Let there be seriousness in this hour. Father, I thank you for everything that you're doing in this region. I thank you for the 5 men whose hearts are saying yes. We will run together. We will form alliance. We will see this state change. We will pour our heart into it. God, your forming, your bringing forth something of The Kingdom out of people who have found their identity. Father, I thank you for these things tonight. I thank you for the strategies and plans that were released and are coming into the earth to bear fruit, to bear down upon us even now.

Father, we thank you for everything you've done in our lives, in our ministry this week. God, I pray for churches throughout this region that there be a fresh anointing in this season, God. God, that pastors would find their identity and God, as they do that, The Kingdom would be released through them. Father, I just thank you for these things tonight, and I bless you, in Jesus name! Amen!

Four Anointings Released

12/16/2006 by Greg Crawford, Apostle

Jubilee International Ministries Ministry Base, Fairfield

This is an exciting thing. This is going to release the next generation. There are going to be prayer furnaces on fire throughout this whole state. You can't ever see something break open, because somebody imports something. It's because there's no investment that comes, because they haven't made a commitment to the land. They're just passing through and they're only under the authority of those of whatever house they are in. They're not under the authority of the men that would be (planted) in a region. So when God's government is established in the state, it's going to release something and bring it to a higher level. It's going to rock some people's world. It's going to confront false doctrine and teaching. It's going to confront things we've allowed in The Church that should never be. It's going to make a standard of holiness and righteousness.

Things are going to be addressed in the spirit realm and they're going to be cut through in a moment of time, cause God doesn't have time in this hour to sit here and try to talk us into believing it. He's just going to start demonstrating it, and let you figure it out later on. All these men went through a lot of demonstration. They were modeling the Kingdom is what they were doing. Not just declaring with their mouth, but they were modeling it. The Iowa Alliance For Reformation we are forming is going to model something of The Kingdom that has probably not been seen. And so in this house, these are the things God is speaking to my heart. My heart is so much on this state, so much of what is going on in this state, for the leaders of this state. But the leaders of this state have to be shaken. There has to be a shaking because there are too many souls at stake. But they don't know where to go and they don't know what to do and nobody's given them any purpose or any destiny or anything. That's sitting inside all of them and it's frustrating the grace of God. That has to shift in this hour. So, that's where we are. That's what is coming.

So, tonight, what I want to share is, I'm literally going to go over last Saturday's message, because we all got blown out of the water. I don't know about you, but I got blown out of the water. I'm trying to digest what God said. People are getting these messages now

Then the Lord started speaking to me about how it's coming into our state, into the four corners. And how the prophecies of Dutch Sheets and Chuck Pierce said we're going to glean the four corners of this state, that four apostles will arise and there will be a completeness of the Gospel that will be coming into this state that we've never seen. The Kingdom is going to be loosed to these four anointings. Then something is going to shift, because these are four anointings for four dynamics of The Kingdom. There is a new dynamic of The Kingdom that we've not yet seen. These things are coming out of that.

So, there are four carpenters. Carpenters are builders. In *Leviticus 25* it talks of the year of Jubilee. That this is going to be a year of coming out of debt and indebtedness. That is not about our physical, natural debt, it is about your spiritual debt, the indebtedness of your spiritual life. It's about coming out of that, we will return to our possessions, not our (earthly) possessions, but our spiritual possessions, what we've let go of. We return to our land, not our physical land, but our spiritual land of influence; our cities, our regions and states and nations. All of these things are coming in this next year and there's a shifting and I haven't even had time to study it, but I know those four dynamics of Kingdom are in jubilee, in *Leviticus 25*. I know they are sitting in there. Those are the reflections of restoration.

All of these men were restorers of a future that hadn't been seen. That is what jubilee does. Jubilee brings a time of restoration and a time of hope of the future that is about to come.

2. Four new Focuses of Intercession

Here's what the Lord spoke to me just this afternoon. That out of this is going to come four distinctions of intercession into the Church. **Enoch, we will intercede as friends of God** knowing that we are a friend. Knowing that He hears us. Having the confidence that what we pray for is surely in our hand. That is the Kingdom as it is, as it is right now. We are a friend of God. We do not have that identity yet, but that identity is coming to you, so that you will realize who you are. What God has created you to do on this earth. Be a friend of God.

A friend knows the secrets of another friend. There is intimacy in that. **Our intercession is coming in to reveal the secrets of God's heart**, and the intimacy as friends. The second thing is **Joseph- interceding as those who have experienced refuge**. Knowing the refuge of God knowing the hiding of God. Knowing that even though everybody may slay me, my God is still for me. Coming into intercession, knowing that we are interceding to bring people into a refuge of His heart, that's a real different way of looking at it, isn't it?

Kingdom now! **Daniel- an interceeder, as one of**

the spokesmen for God. Knowing what is on His heart that He wants to declare. Not just what is on His heart, but what He wants to actually declare into the earth realm. That is where He was. That is the Kingdom future.

Isaiah- an intercessor as a reformer. God is going to start making us pray in a way that brings reformation into the earth. Not just a revival, I'm sick of revival. No revival, I want awakening! I want reformation. Revival means to get back to the state that we are supposed to be having. Awakening means we're going to a place where something's being revealed to our spirit that has never been revealed. Reformation is about reforming everything so society embraces the awakening of God's heart. Those are the things that God wants to do in intercession. So, with that, we ought to start tonight.

3. Enoch Dynamics

We go to *Hebrews 11:5* There's so much in the Bible about Enoch. If you start looking, you'll find some more things. *"By faith, Enoch was translated that He should not see death; and was not found, because God has translated him; for before his translation he has this testimony, that he pleased God."* You see, last week, I talked about it, that he saw the Kingdom as it is. He was anointed to go into the revelatory realm. He was to transition humanity into the third heaven, and he was building a relationship with God. And I expanded on some of that. Well, let's talk about Enoch. "He pleased God!" The word 'pleased' is only used three times in scriptures. It's used twice in talking about Enoch in reference to Enoch, and one other time about people who are walking according to righteousness. It's not used any other time in scriptures.

Enoch was the father of Methuselah. Methuselah was the name the Lord gave me 3 years ago, and He said "There's something about Methuselah that you've got to understand." Methuselah was his son, and when Methuselah was born, Enoch thought (where am I getting this?) I've read Enoch and the Watchers, I read the historical documents and I've read Josephus and I've been reading and reading, reading on stuff. There is a lot of historical documentation and it gives us understanding of things. Do you realize that Enoch is quoted 24 times in the New Testament? You see, we're scared to read a book like that. Because it's not the Bible, but we'll quote anybody off the bookshelf today. Yet, Jesus and Paul and Peter all quoted Enoch, and they quoted him 24 times. So Enoch had a son born, Methuselah. When he was born, his face was aglow and his eyes a flame of fire. So much like an angel, he said he had the appearance like an angel. So he named him Methuselah, which means 'who is of God'. He lived longer than any man on the face of the earth. The Lord spoke to me and he said, **this anointing that is coming is going to birth that which is eternal. It is going to birth that which is of God.** As the Enoch anointing is loosed in the earth**, there is the appearance of God coming into the earth** that has not appeared as yet. It will be the glow of the glory of God upon faces and the fire of God within the eyes of men, **There will be a shining force of what is birthed this year.** Enoch saw all kinds of things, He saw how the whole spiritual realm held the earth realm together. He saw the angels that were in charge of every dynamic. Angels that were in charge of rivers and streams and the wind, but he also saw the angels in charge of the oaths and vows that men took. He saw angels that were in charge of judgment and justice, of loosing and binding. He saw angels that were in charge of regions of the earth, and have been given authority over some of the affairs of men to loose things in men's lives, so men would grow in the spirit realms into righteousness. He saw angels in charge of decrees of God that men would decree and if we've got ourselves lined up, we've got angels moving on the decree we've just made. When you make a vow, and you pay your tithe, or, if you don't pay your tithe, guess what? You just moved an angel who's in charge of oaths and vows. There's an angel in charge, one way or the other. Enoch also saw Seraphim and Cherubim and he also saw Ophannim. - a third one. I've never seen that in scripture, where did you find that? Oh, but if you dig a little bit, here's what it means, it actually means 'the wheels of Ezekiel' personified, he saw the things we keep praying to see, but we never can see. A wheel within a wheel, and eyes, and multifaceted things. It's in *Ezekiel 1:10* if you want to know where it's at. **What he saw was those things that are making declaration in heaven**. We're talking about Enoch anointing tonight. It's wild, isn't it? We won't just know assignments, but we will be burdened with the same things that are burdening the heart of God tonight. It will drive us to sacrifice and pay any price, go anywhere, and do anything. We're not there yet because we have not identified with it. **Enoch was a model of intercession to spare the earth**. God spoke to him, spoke to him and spoke to him. He came back and he talked about righteousness and righteousness being established. God finally said, Enoch, I'm sending you home for one year to rest and one year to speak to your descendants and then I'm taking you home. I'm going to flood the earth and I'm going to wipe it out because you've gone and you've spoken and you've gone and spoken and nothing has changed.

That will come out of this as well. That will be the chaos that will arise. It will be the flood that my wife saw. That will be those things that are coming. Kind of exciting, isn't it? **Enoch means 'dedicated one'**

and that's what it's gonna take to be a friend of God. A friend of God is one that has to have their life dedicated in intimacy. This is the season where God is not playing games any more. This is the season where the forerunners are forerunning this next thing into the face of the earth, and it's gonna come with some scarring and some sacrifice, some battles. It's going to come with some intensity, but it's going to come with joy, intimacy, a reviewing of the things of God that we have never seen and an understanding of who God is and how God wants to be in our lives. I just love the things about Enoch. Remember I said last week, it's all about miracles that superceded time and space. That's where it's coming to. This thing is going to supercede a lot of things.

4. Joseph Dynamics

Seeing the Kingdom in the now, Joseph's anointing was another time and season. The sons of Issachar, (son of Jacob and Leah) came out of Joseph. It was about the transforming of a nation and building a place of refuge. Remember Joseph had a dream in his heart and his identity was the word already put inside of him. In *Psalm 105*, it says the Word tried him. There was the trying of the Word of God that was sitting inside of him and those were some of the things we talked about last week. So, tonight we're going to talk about some other things.

Joseph's life was saved by Reuben and Reuben was the first born of Israel. **The first born is the one that shifts the things in family units. The generation that is coming up is going to be the one of the first born into Kingdom dynamics of modeling of spiritual fathering and mothering. It is going to be the one that will save the others. Joseph was raised in Hebron, he was raised in a place of alliance** until he was sold out of alliance into Egypt. When Jacob died, he said what? I want my bones buried back at Hebron at the place of Alliance.

Out of Joseph, came two sons, Ephraim and Manasseh. We talked about it at conference this past time. **Ephraim means 'double ash heap and double fruitfulness'.**

Manasseh means ' being allowed to be forgotten'. In *Genesis 41:51*, he named him Manasseh because he said this "The Lord has made me forget my toil". No longer toiling in this, I'm no longer laboring and the Lord spoke to me and said **'when this Joseph anointing is released, the toiling and laboring of ministry will cease**. It will come effortlessly.' We will forget the days of the past and the struggles that we have had. Cause it will fade in the glory that is coming upon us. Like Enoch's son, Methuselah, with glory coming upon the face and eyes, the flame of fire, the passion of God burning in our hearts so great that everything will pale in comparison to what we see God doing in front of us this next year. This is going to be an exciting year! **We're going to be put in a place of multiplication.**

I'll tell you why this is important. Because, this generation that is coming up has a dream in their heart and they've been put in a pit with no water. They've been put in a place of a dungeon. They've been put here. They've been put there. Discarded, but God is about to bring them out. **Because the dream in their heart is also connected to Ephraim and Manasseh who made the alliance at Hebron with David.**

It was the Hebron alliance that is being formed by men in this state, in this hour. We are coming into the place we're indebted, we're in distress, we're in despair and we don't know what to do, but we can't be in the cave any more. **The dream is too big that's in our hearts and the dream that in the next generation of Manassehs and Ephraims is too big.** They are not a double ash heap. They are to be double fruitfulness. They are not to be forgotten. **Their name shall be in the roll call and the alliance with David shall be made.** This is the shift that is coming next year. Joseph was known for knowing the times and seasons and the interpretation of dreams That is the sign of kairos and chronos of God, that timing of

God and the divine moments of God. **It is about the release of storehouses.** In *Genesis 41:57*, there is a storehouse anointing coming to the church to release the corn to the nations.

This is a direct prophecy related to what Dutch Sheets and Chuck Pierce said. That we will flow with corn, oil and wine and we are flowing with the corn and wine, because we've got the vineyards established, but we've got the oil thing still coming. What this is, **this is an anointing to release revelatory truth because the interpretation of dreams was revelatory to reveal what was hidden, so men could plan their futures.** That came out of Joseph's life. This is also about **administration of the Kingdom and how we do administration concerning the kingdom.** I'll tell you where it's coming from. We've talked about next generation and we've talked about the upcoming generation.

I'll tell you why this is coming. It's coming because some Jacobs have wrestled for the blessings of God not knowing what blessings they needed. But there was a season yet to draw upon it. Did he not wrestle all night and said, 'God, you must bless me'? He wrestled until the hollow of his thigh was touched but was he wrestling for a present tense blessing? **He was wrestling for a future tense blessing that would come one day that his whole family could survive.**

The next generation gets the blessing but there's one who paid the price of wrestling, so you can get the blessing in this hour. What is happening with Joseph anointing being released is only a manifestation of what the past generations have wrestled for, so you can have your blessing in this season. That is what this is about. It is about the fulfillment. **It is about showing honor to who has paid the price they have paid.**

5. Isaiah Dynamics

Isaiah saw the Kingdom in the beginning. He was anointed to declare the Kingdom. A reformer of mindsets established the mountain to build the house. When he saw the throne of God in *Isaiah 6*.

Everyone needs an Isaiah 6 encounter; I've had one. I've had an *Ezekiel 37* encounter and *Ezekiel 47* encounter. You've got to go after these encounters with God. That is the thing that has launched me into ministry. It's the thing that makes me have a passion for the state. It is that I've had some encounters. Those are the things to get you through some hard times. He prophesied for 64 years to a nation that really didn't want to hear it. Reforming some things. Other prophets were on the scene. They were speaking things that move mindsets. Isaiah was a reformer.

Here's what the Lord spoke to me today. This is pretty deep! You have to grab it. *Revelation 10:6-7 And sware by him that liveth for ever and ever, who created heaven, and the things that therein are, and the earth, and the things that therein are, and the sea, and the things which are therein, that there should be time no longer: 7 But in the days of the voice of the seventh angel, when he shall begin to sound, the mystery of God should be finished, as he hath declared to his servants the prophets.* Vs. 11- *And he said unto me, Thou must prophesy again before many peoples, and nations, and tongues, and kings.*

We've covered this before, and it means **to prophesy anew.** Here's what God spoke to me. "Because of Joseph's anointing, and knowing the times and seasons, we will prophesy anew, not declaring the future, but prophesying the finishing anointing that has been loosed." Sitting right here in this state, Dutch Sheets spoke it at Council Bluffs, IA this year. He said. **There is a finishing anointing sitting upon the state of Iowa to finish what God has started to birth inside of them. We're not going to be prophesying our future and keep prophesying the future because there comes a day where the future is no more, it is now!** There is a finishing anointing for us to start prophesying and decreeing the pulling of the future into the new movement of God, so something is established in this moment. This day is not waiting for something to come in days and days and months and years, and hang the carrot in front of the horse. (Where are these analogies coming from, God?) But, there is a finishing anointing to prophesy anew. I hope you get that! It's hinging you see these things are hinging. Out of Joseph, came Issachar, the son of Jacob and Leah. Issachar, who knew the times and seasons. You prophesy the same old thing and you just give the same old word in the same old way. When you start knowing the time and seasons, it's like this message tonight for some of you, you've never heard anybody speak like this. It is because I know the time and seasons coming into this state. So, I'm preaching it the way God wants to preach this thing. See! This thing is coming for us to finish this.

Isaiah is one of the greatest hope books there is and what is coming is hope that has never been seen before. But not prophesying hope in the future, prophesying the finishing of it in people's lives. That is reformation that is touching some things. *Isaiah 2:2-3 And it shall come to pass in the last days, that the mountain of the LORD'S house shall be established in the top of the mountains, and shall be exalted above the hills; and all nations shall flow unto it. 3 And many people shall go and say, Come ye, and let us go up to the mountain of the LORD, to the house of the God of Jacob; and he will teach us of his ways, and we will walk in his paths: for out of Zion shall go forth the law, and the word of the LORD from Jerusalem.* Establishing the mountain to build the house is the key. It is the key!

Here's what the Lord spoke to me: **"The next two years will finish the establishing of the mountain and end the seven year war of Saul."** We are starting the sixth year of the seven-year war of Saul. The structure of Saul is being torn down and shifted. It will take this alliance running through this state for two years to see this thing come and establish it. This is not going to happen in three months, six months or a year. We have to be in this for the long haul. And if you're not, you had better not even get started at the beginning. This thing is going to cost to do it and do it right. We have to be in it to see it finished. Not half way, cause the Church has been known for going half way and not finishing any wall like Nehemiah built. We have to be like Nehemiah on the wall and say 'I'm doing a great work and I can't come down this moment to hear your pettiness." We have to get on with the program cause there's something that has to be built inside the wall. It's about building a new structure for God to contain something and I'm not saying, we are going out of here and building a bunch of churches and stuff. I'm saying, we're building a container of the Body of Christ to hold the Glory of God and the face of Methuselah can come upon us.

6. **Daniel Dynamics**

Daniel saw the Kingdom in the future and was

anointed to be a spokesman for God. Transitioning a nation is what his goal was! **His agenda was in his heart cause He said, he would safeguard it. He wouldn't turn aside,** He wouldn't indulge himself in the things of the world. Here's what I want us to understand; Daniel shifted his current age by bringing a future age in. That is what was going to be released in this Daniel anointing. **We are bringing a future age of the church into this present age.** He shifted it when He was thrown into the lion's den and the lions didn't devour him because he shifted out of that age to another age. He was translated like Enoch and like Isaiah. That's why Isaiah was translated into the throne room of God. What he went through did not touch his life. **He released a strategy. Here's what I want you to hear; he released a strategy to build the house of God.** You see, **Isaiah released a strategy to establish it, but Daniel released the strategy to build it.** We're all thinking about physical things, right now, but it's spiritual.   In Daniel 2:35- He saw what Isaiah saw about the mountain being established. He was all about building God's house and the defilement of the house itself even when Nebuchadnezzar took the golden goblets out of the house of God. Do you realize that for the first time in history, a Gentile was the king? It's terrible! There was a breach in the tabernacle of David, and he begged God and prayed. There was an intercession that he did for a nation. See there was a shifting in these things. He begged God and prayed. He said, God, shift this nation, but see the house built back. Let's see the glory come back in the way it's supposed to be. He cried out for it., stood and said, "I will not compromise for what I believe. I will not shift off this place, where God is first place in my life." He was about accuracy in the spirit realm here's these guys drinking out of these golden goblets and here comes the handwriting on the wall and the knees of Nebuchadnezzar are literally shaking where people can hear. What did he hear? He brought the reverence of God back into the house. Sitting there touching holy vessels when you shouldn't be touching them. Doing things that you shouldn't be doing. What does he say to Nebuchadnezzar eventually? Guess what Buddy? You're gonna wander around and eat grass, you're gonna get scales like feathers on your body and you're gonna get claws and you're going to look like a mad man running around. **It's wisdom of God to know the mysteries of God, what's going to be released in coming.** Ananias and Sapphira are coming. There's a shifting coming in the spring where God's not gonna play. The games are done. That is finished There is a seriousness in this hour and it is coming. Until there is true repentance in the hearts of people, they will either be removed or replaced. **What did Daniel do? He modeled the Kingdom in front of all kingdoms.** He didn't voice it with words; he modeled it with his life. I will not bow to that image and if you throw me into the fire, you throw me into the fire. I love that; there were four men in the fire including the Son of God. **What's being released is the wisdom of God.**

Knowing what has been sealed because what has been sealed has only been concealed. Not that we don't have access in, God is going to start bringing wisdom because what was Daniel known for? He was known for wisdom beyond his years. **This next generation is coming with wisdom of how to confront kingdoms. It's going to be wisdom that will influence current leaders.** I've already heard a testimony about that today. Daniel didn't confront that which was false, but interpreted correctly what was false and let truth confront it. We're letting the enemy's plans effect how we plan our life and what we do and how we should rally and why we should call a meeting. You see Daniel said, here's truth and truth is what's going to confront it. I don't confront it, I model the Kingdom with my life. **But I let the truth of how things are interpreted confront that, which is false.** That is why there is a shift in doctrine right now, that we would really get truth inside of us and speak the same thing. We can't speak multiple things and expect something to shift. People want to tag along, just to look and see. You can't tag along and you can't speak the thing you'll be a detriment to this. I didn't get too many amens on that deal. Here's what prophesying anew is, actually it's gonna reach the point where it is modeling the prophecy. You see what I'm saying? It is where we model it as the fulfillment of it. I thought Jesus was the spirit of prophecy. The testimony of Jesus was the spirit of prophecy. His spirit was prophecy. His life was a prophecy. Isn't it interesting that Enoch is quoted 24 times but Daniel has 24 prophecies fulfilled There are two statements and I'm' done.

7. Four Kingdom Dynamics Common Ground

All four men were royal lineage and you're of royal lineage, holy priesthood and very peculiar people. All four saw a king and a kingdom that they could identify. That explained their function and **they went out and functioned in what they saw**. Isn't it interesting, there is so much about these four lives that we've got to study out in this hour to see what is coming. So you see tonight, we come in here and this is a meeting for the region, this is not a church meeting. You are The Church or the Ekklesia of the ruling ones that govern and rule the laws of society. That is what you're supposed to do with your life. Church is not a building or a place or act of time. Church is a living, breathing, effective organism controlled by the Spirit of God and voiced by Him. With passion in your hearts and the tenacity to engage and confront anything. That is who you are. I'm so excited about this; I'm counting the days until this state is changed.

Greg Crawford

Chapter 5

Not Abandoning Our Prophetic Journey

By now you can see the unbelievable promise God has given us for our state. In many ways, we have a large responsibility in not just seeing these things come to pass for our sakes but also for the nation. Iowa has been a key place in God's heart since its statehood. He has seen it as playing a major role in His overall plan for our nation. I put it this way- we must finish what God has declared because the nation is hinging on it.

We need to see things through the eyes of God. If He declared these things and they have been in His heart, then He also has a means for them to be fulfilled. He has special grace and anointing just for us as a state. He also has a prophetic destiny that is awaiting us.

I pray we do not repeat the patterns of the past, especially during the time of the Iowa Band. In many ways, we are at the same cross roads again. Current prophetic voices have said we are a revelatory state and that we are going to increase in population. These are similarities that we had with our forerunners 150 years ago. I pray our decisions will have a different outcome.

One of the main things I see as a pattern that seems to be key in shifting all things is fresh revelation. It is what shifted things biblically and is what is needed today. We need to find the streams of revelation that have been opened in our state and begin to figure out how to feed the nation from these divine resources God has given.

Revelation always requires a response and a corresponding action. We see this in our history of the Iowa Band. When the reception stopped, so did the Church's function. It also causes us to reexamine our priorities and our value systems. It might actually begin to touch our belief systems and wrong doctrine.

It seems Iowa is posed to be a model to the nation. This is quite an honor and also some pretty uncharted territory. The pioneer type spirit is still present in Iowa. It looks different than the early settlers. They depended on each other and faced new obstacles. Today we are too independent as a people and basically try to go it alone. The pioneering spirit of old is what is truly needed today.

As a state, we have a rich resource in our young people as well. They have a destiny and currently are looking for a cause. When we talk about shifting a state or our nation, we cannot in any way overlook our emerging generations. After all, they must be involved in the process now to have ownership in the future. The bulk of those who traveled the state in the Iowa Alliance meetings were primarily young people. They need to know what they are hooking up with is real and will last. If presented these two things, then they will not abandon their prophetic destiny as well.

As I look at all the Lord has spoken over our state, I believe He is not going to give up on us or back down for one second. I believe He is looking for who would be willing to go on this prophetic journey with Him and see His hand move through their life. Reformation is a large undertaking and so is awakening, yet both will come whether we participate with or oppose them.

Iowa, the Land between two rivers, the place artists came to see the handiwork and creativity of God. Let's move forward into our future and bring back this same creative flow again into our state. Let us work together to see the Kingdom of God come and the 150-year-old mandate of the Iowa Band fulfilled so Iowa would be a state "the reformers would come from".

Chapter 6

The Journey Continues

By now a lot of time has passed since this book was first written. Many changes have occurred both personally and in the ministry concerning the state of Iowa. I felt the need to add some new chapters as some things have unfolded and more things are in process. I have tried not to include prophetic words concerning the ministry of the BASE even though its primary call is state wide awakening. I have tried to include as many prophetic words as I am aware of. After the first writing, I had some upset that I did not include their actions in what they did in their cities. The reason was it was more specific for a ministry and not really a state wide word.

First let me say the ministry did make the move from Fairfield to the capital, Des Moines under God's direction. It was a supernatural move with 25 people relocating to Des Moines. We had to sell our 28,000 sq. foot building, establish a new location, sell homes, quit jobs and then find new homes and jobs. Moving from a small town to a metro city was also a cultural adjustment. At this time, everything is settled with the BASE ministry and we are now active again in a focus on the state.

I will not tell of the gatherings of the pockets from across the state nor the many connections made with those we have found contending in different areas of Iowa. I will say the first change of significance is the state capital. We immediately got involved in the prayer group there and began to influence the type of praying and greatly shifted things. After 8 years, we now have a prayer group of legislators formed who pray for the people of Iowa. We have seen the Governor proclaim a day of prayer and the Bible read at the courthouses of Iowa. These things are touching all of the state.

As for a ministry, we are finding hungry ones in Iowa and beginning to find the pace of things. We also have connected with awakening groups in the nation and have a strong voice in Kentucky who is going through the beginning stages of awakening. In all honesty, we seemed to be closer to connecting and moving as one a few years ago. That was when the apostolic was the new phrase being used. There was a season of considering the apostolic but it was not embraced. There has been a great lull of very little activity of truly coming together as five-fold leaders. There are still pastoral gatherings but no real recognition of apostolic leaders. Some may assume they are apostolic, but are not really functioning as such. The three stages of apostolic calling, commissioning and apostleship are not really understood nor is apostolic grace. Mainly at this time it's more about having a checklist than an apostolic lifestyle based in grace. The embracing of apostles and prophets in Kentucky has advanced them greatly into being positioned to see a genuine move of God come. There is a large amount of interacting and cross pollination of leaders working towards a common purpose. This is coming from apostolic influences and prophetic input being embraced. These are two key components needed in Iowa. Also the need to pray into existence the prophetic words and promises God has given to us. As a ministry, we have pressed hard into this for close to 20 years. We have seen some come to pass and others are in different stages of completion. The number of state focused words have been very lacking as well. Here are some more prophetic words to mobilize around.

A New Birth of Freedom
Greg Crawford   May 2010

I had a night visitation from the Lord that was very unique in scope and assignment. He spoke to me and said "The message for 'Awakening Fires Arising' (our first state wide gathering in Des Moines) is written inside the state capitol on the wall. Go there tomorrow and I will show you". I woke up in the morning and began pouring over all the prophetic words for Iowa. I re-read 'Iowa's Prophetic Journey' especially the words Dutch Sheets and Chuck Pierce spoke. After lunch, my wife and I went to the capitol on our Kingdom assignment.

Upon arriving, we began to read every plaque, story and piece of paper our eyes could find. We went into the House chambers, the law library and of course, the Rotunda. I was drawn to a large silver bell by the model ship of the U.S.S. Iowa. For some reason, I felt it had significance but there wasn't much writing with it and the Lord said what I was looking for was "written on the wall". I had gotten the impression it was His hand that had written it much like the writing on the wall that Daniel interpreted. It was something sovereign that had been placed by the Lord.

We moved to the top of the Rotunda, looking at pictures of angels and other things. As I climbed the steps of the Rotunda and looked backward, there it was at the top of the wall between two columns. "a new birth of Freedom" . This was quickened to my spirit that this was the writing on the wall as I suddenly realized it was in the exact location I had seen in a dream in the night. As I moved on around, I found the context of the writing. "This nation under God shall have a new birth of Freedom". The Lord said "This will be the rallying message for Iowa". The writing continues to encircle the rotunda with "of government by the people for the people shall not perish under the earth."

I returned home and began to continue reading the prophetic words Dutch and Chuck had spoken over Iowa. Within a few minutes, I came across the confirmation. "So I bring Jubilee into the land and let the oppressed go free – to set at liberty the broken and bruised. I want to restore! I want to let captives go free! I want somebody to go throughout the land and say, "Freedom! Liberty! Ring the bell of freedom!" Now I had the meaning of the silver bell I was drawn to. The sound of redemption, the sound of freedom. A new birth of Freedom for the Church of Iowa!

As the Awakening Fires Arising meeting began, the Lord spoke to me and said "I placed the writing on the wall like I placed the stones in the stream for David. I knew My Church would need a new sense of freedom one day and I wrote it on the wall years ago knowing I could call upon someone to access it in this hour and begin to proclaim it." He then began to speak that as I shared about this new birth of freedom that it was for the nation but was to start here in our state of Iowa. That this was the rallying call He wanted to speak from our state capitol which was placed so no man could take credit for it and something everyone who went to the state capitol could experience and be reminded of when they read the writing on the wall.

The Lord went on to say that this day He was going to bring a different type of healing. It would be a healing of anything that was hindering freedom, a deep freedom to be expressed. This new birth of freedom would be so radical it would be like being born again, but born into freedom. That The Church was lacking true freedom and needed a radical experience in it. He also spoke to me and said that this freedom that would be birthed in Iowa would affect the nation as well. He showed me that even the location of the writing in our state capitol, the heart of the nation would go outward and affect the nation. It was like the words I saw were pulsing within my spirit.

As the Awakening Fires Arising meeting unfolded, I had a chance to share this and minister out of this unique visitation. I shared the events that you just read and how the Lord led me in this unique path. We came to a place in the meeting that the Lord wanted to minister healing in what was stopping freedom by depositing the seeds of freedom within people. No prayer line was needed, just a yielded heart. This was a sovereign thing happening in our midst. We asked the Lord for the Holy Spirit to show us those things stopping our freedom in our individual lives. The Holy Spirit spoke to people and began to remove and replace each thing with seeds of freedom. I could sense such a deep thing in the Spirit I had no words to describe the depth of what was occurring. I was even wondering at the time of God's imparting: 'Do we really know the depth of this?' Does everyone really get what God is doing in us and through us to launch awakening into our state and even our nation? A new birth of freedom! Amongst the multitude of things shared by so many, the visions and prophetic words, etc., Adam Larson had a vision while I was speaking and saw an angel of the Lord standing and throwing seeds into the hearts of people. He said it was the seeds of the new birth of freedom. Testimonies were asked for and about 75% of the people got up in some fashion and testified of the deposit of freedom that was made. Some with great tears. Some who never speak at an open mic. It was truly an amazing thing to see and witness. God has sovereignly and solidly given the rallying call of the awakening for the state of Iowa that will also affect the nation. The seeds of new freedom will begin to grow and so will the impact into the state. This indeed is the "precious seed to be scattered across the prairie" prophesied over my life in 1995 that would occur. This is the fulfillment of God's heart, someone ring the freedom bell! This is the rally call for Iowa's awakening "This nation under God shall have **a new birth of Freedom!"** It had already started in Iowa on June 5th, 2010!

Burning the Cornfields
Darrin Begley   July 2014

"God says I'm burning for you. I'm coming to burn your religious cornfields up. And in the middle of burning them up, I'm going to expose that spirit that thinks that the field belongs to them and has been in control so they have thought. For this state is a state to prophesy to this nation. In 2008, this state prophesied to the nation and they did not receive your prophecy." (Iowa Caucus) But God says "I am shifting it. And even starting now this state will start to prophesy to the nation, but they will hear your words 8 years later when they rejected it. For as my fire comes to burn up the religious cornfields, the dormant seed that has been laying underneath will now start to come forth. And it will be a new crop, of a new generation that will not have the stench of religion around them". So God says "get ready and prepare for harvest", for what looked like God's denial was just His delay for this time.

Darrin then went on to give the BASE some very specific words. I won't give the details here as I'm trying to keep this book to include everyone in the state. What was pertinent to the state is; we are to travel through the state again, that an army of young people will rise, that more revelation will be published from Iowa and that the key to much of it will be spiritual fathering.

Build a Throne in Iowa
Greg Crawford   Dec 2014

The Lord spoke to me a couple months ago and said to me, "I want you to build My throne in Iowa." I was a little surprised by the words and thought *'who am I to do such a thing? There is no way I can build God's throne, only He can do that'*. But it took me on a journey to try to discover exactly what God was saying to me. Was it a type and shadow, was it literal or did it have a hidden meaning?

Hebrews 4:16 (KJV 1900) — 16 Let us therefore come boldly unto the throne of grace, that we may obtain mercy, and find grace to help in time of need.

For starters, a throne is a place of ultimate rule. It is a point of governing and also decrees. It is representative of a nation, country, or a group of people. God's throne is a place of divine power and final authority. God's throne is a place of grace. Not just grace in the normal understanding of saving grace or redemptive grace, but all graces associated with the seven natures of Christ found in **Isaiah 11:2-3.** So to build a throne is to build grace. Paul came to the point of stewarding grace in **Ephesians 3:1-3** when he said he was given a dispensation of grace. So a throne is a place of dispensing grace as well. The grace is sitting waiting on someone to activate it …. The nature of God in us is the catalyst!

The throne is also sovereign and represents the sovereignty of God. It is what everything in heaven and earth is revolving around. It is also a place that is supporting the One seated. It is not so much a chair like we imagine seeing a king sitting, but a place of resting upon grace. When the Bible speaks of God's "throne", the emphasis is on God's transcendence, His dignity, and sovereign rule. The fact that His throne is in heaven further underscores the transcendent nature of God's existence.

The word 'transcendence' means "to exist above and independent from; to rise above, surpass, succeed." Being transcendent, God is both the unknown and unknowable, yet God continually seeks to reveal Himself to His creation. In other words, the unknown seeks to be known. This transcendent nature that places Him beyond the reach of His creation is His holiness and His righteousness. So the throne to build will exist separated and apart from all the other thrones. It will not be associated with manmade thrones and kingdoms but will be above it. It will surpass that which is currently being seen.

So I have begun to realize I can't actually build a throne as we would know it, but I can build the things around the throne and also dispense the grace that comes from that throne. How strange of us to look at Moses' tabernacle and David's tabernacle and go back and try to copy these things, when God said He would build His tabernacle as He desired. In Hebrews, it talks about the patterns of heaven and its reflection on the earth. Perhaps we should be building according to the heavenly pattern instead of copying a past earthly pattern.

Let me begin by sharing a vision I had of the throne. I have had several throne room visitations and I will only speak of the most recent one. I was in a meeting in Paducah, Kentucky with Prophet David Kelly and Freedom Center. During the worship, I had a vision of the throne with Jesus seated there. I knew the vision would be part of my journey and I also had a sense it was for the guest speaker, John Alley, an Apostle from Australia. I found out later just how far reaching this vision was.

In this vision, I was taken to the throne. Jesus was seated there and before Him were five steps representing grace. A large stone table was before Him just beyond the bottom step. On this stone table were two large scrolls. Each was a single scroll with handles on both ends. The paper in the middle was not really paper but was liquid granite which was spinning. These scrolls seemed to be available to anyone wishing to reach out for them.

I saw the Lord bend over while seated and lift the scroll on His right. When He did, the fiery spinning granite would continue to spin and suddenly a tongue of fire would come out several feet protruding in the direction of the other scroll. When it went out, it then would become solid granite and had writing on it that could be seen from the throne. The Lord would begin to drop the scroll and the tongue of granite would repel back into the fiery spinning scroll. The Lord would pick up the other scroll and in the same manner it would all occur again protruding towards the other scroll. Then He would place that scroll down on the stone table as well.

He would lean backward and simply call for the scroll. He was calling for it because He wanted to stay at rest. The scroll He called for would lift from the table and begin to fly around the throne all ablaze and spinning. It would come into His hand and then He raised it. The Lord said, "When you raise this scroll in your hand, it will become a living scepter by which to rule from." Then He would release the scroll and it would fly and return. The second scroll repeated through this process and the same words of it being a living scepter were spoken when He raised it.

Then I saw the Lord reach down to the table and pick up both scrolls at once. The tongues of fire came forth just like before but now the two joined in the middle and interlocked. They became hard like granite again and I could hear the angels say "you can stand on this now". The words appeared on each scroll and when they came together in the middle, they became a single sentence to be read. I knew this meant a seamless grace could be found in the Old and New Testaments. God was showing me something of great magnitude about the throne, His seven graces, His seven natures and what He desired to bring forth.

In the vision, I knew I could take the far handle and lift the scroll at any time as well and it would become solid with writing. The throne is knowing the time and seasons and also the intentions of God. It also is declaring with all boldness the scepter of His Word, ruling with that Word and allowing that Word to be the flaming sword by which we rule. It is the place where the priests of God who carry His nature release His expression. These priests are beginning to be woven into a single garment and covering for our state. They are a remnant, a holy community, a covering much like the covering of these flying flaming scrolls. They have been set aside to handle the holy things of God. The flaming spinning whirlwinds of heaven's scroll. These priests will rule and reign and decree with all authority standing on the Word as they read a seamless grace. They will steward that grace seeing the new wineskin of Sonship being birthed to hold the new wine of Holy Community.

Before I go to the heart of the revelation of building the throne, let me simply list some things about the throne. We all know that Moses saw the throne of God and the sea of glass. He was able to take seventy elders into that same vision so they could receive the same Spirit. That same Spirit was the nature of God and the graces with that nature. Moses asked the Lord if he had found "grace" (the age of grace) and God said no, as it had not yet been given. David saw the same things concerning the throne and asked the same question and got the same answer. Now today we are stuck on redemptive grace and do not even associate that the throne has multiple graces to draw from. Isaiah saw the throne as well and saw the train or mantel of a high priest filling the temple. This is symbolic of apostolic covering or mantling to insure consecration, abundance, and accomplishment coming forth.

The following characteristics are what God is building. It is descriptive of having holy community with each other and esteeming each other. It is descriptive of graces that we can draw from at different times.

- **God's throne is a place of power and authority.** In **II Chronicles 18:18**, the prophet Micah relates his vision of God's throne room, in which spirit beings stand in attendance. It is a place of God's rule.
- **God's throne is a place of majesty and honor.** The Bible says that when Jesus ascended to heaven, He "sat down at the right hand of the throne of God" (**Hebrews 12:2**). There is no higher place than heaven. God is the King of heaven, and Jesus holds the place of honor at God's right hand. So it is a place of honor and esteeming each other like the Godhead does. The throne is a place of non-competiveness and a place of valuing each as an individual and all as a collective.
- **God's throne is a place of perfect justice.** "He has prepared His throne for judgment" **Psalm 4:7**. Justice will prevail when God's throne is in place. This is the place of imprecatory prayer and coming before the courts of heaven to petition that decisions be rendered.
- **God's throne is a place of sovereignty and holiness.** "God reigns over the nations; God is seated on His holy throne" **Psalm 47:8**.

The throne has always been in place and will forever be in place. It is the ultimate rule full of mercy and grace and full of judgment and righteousness.

- **God's throne is a place of praise.** John's vision of heaven includes a scene in which a "new song" is sung in praise to the One who occupies the throne. **Rev. 5.** The creative dimensions of God are endless.

- **God's throne is a place of purity.** Only the redeemed, those who have been granted the righteousness of Christ, will have the right to stand before His throne.

- **Rev 14:5. God's throne is a place of eternal life. A life giving flow. Rev. 22:1** The throne radiates this life as He holds all things in His hands.

- **God's throne is a place of grace.** Not only does the throne of God represent judgment for the unbeliever, but it also represents mercy and grace for His children. "Let us then approach God's throne of grace with confidence, so that we may receive mercy and find grace to help us in our time of need" **Heb. 14:16**. It is not just a singular grace but is full of graces.

- **God's throne is a meeting place of the elders. Rev. 4:10-11** Before the throne, the sea of glass is in motion. It is the meeting place of heaven. This is where the elders are seated on their thrones and the place they bow down and cast their crowns.

Now this is quite a list and not all inclusive by any means. So what does it mean to build a throne? All I know is the throne is everything we see in heaven which included specifically everything around the throne as well.

Now with the foundation laid, I will begin to unfold the revelation of building the throne of God in Iowa. I will give a rather lengthy portion to unfold the revelation in one writing. Please read **Rev. 4 and 5.**

Revelation 4:1–3 (KJV 1900) — 1 After this I looked, and, behold, a door was opened in heaven: and the first voice which I heard was as it were of a trumpet talking with me; which said, Come up hither, and I will shew thee things which must be hereafter. 2 And immediately I was in the spirit: and, behold, a throne was set in heaven, and one sat on the throne. 3 And he that sat was to look upon like a jasper and a sardine stone: and there was a rainbow round about the throne, in sight like unto an emerald.

The trumpet is sounding in this hour. The word

'trumpet' is connected to a beckoning by reverberation. There is a coming together by the frequencies of heaven moving in our midst. This reverberation is the spiritual reflections of the throne itself. It is the graces flowing outward beckoning us inward. There is the need of things we have not seen yet but God is now showing these things to us.

Revelation 4:5 (KJV 1900) — 5 And out of the throne proceeded lightnings and thunderings and voices: and there were seven lamps of fire burning before the throne, which are the seven Spirits of God.

The Lord had given me a word about a year ago concerning the lightning and thunder. He said "the thundering is my prophets as they speak with My rumblings in the distance to hear. They always signal the storm of My presence before it appears. The Apostles are My lightening. They signal the storm is upon you. They strike fast and illuminate. They pierce darkness and bring heavens frequency to earth."

The voices are the remnant ones who are speaking Kingdom language. They too, are needed in this hour. The seven lamps burning are the seven graces of God. The seven spirits are the seven natures of God. Notice the apostles, prophets and voices are coming out of the throne. The graces and natures are before the throne. God will rise up a new generation of apostles and prophets from where His throne is established. These voices will go through the graces (lamps) and natures (spirits of God). They will be ones to carry these to the earth. Iowa, get ready for a new breed of apostles, prophets and voices to emerge carrying a heavy weight of presence and graces to influence.

So what we are building are the elements around the throne. We have tried to copy earthly patterns of David's tabernacle while yet the pattern is in heaven, the book of Hebrews explains. The elements seen there are the elements needed here. After all, we want God to descend and dwell, so this must have some similarity to the throne there. I'm not stating we set up an actual throne like Dowie did in Zion, Ill. But I am saying we need the elements.

Revelation 4:6 (KJV 1900) — 6 And before the throne there was a sea of glass like unto crystal: and in the midst of the throne, and round about the throne, were four beasts full of eyes before and behind.

The throne is radiating glory --- glory across our state --- a frequency that comes from heavenly sounds being captured and reflected just like this sea that is like crystal. Iowa- we are to reflect these sounds. The sea of glass, the meeting place of heaven, captures all the sounds, colors and reflections. It is a place of motion and the only way we can truly reflect it is if we are in motion. We must build a sea of glass in our meetings. We must build meeting places before the throne across our state. We must build a place that the elders on this sea before the throne can begin to rule. Once we build this reflection, it will enable it to move all of heaven into the earth.

These elders are both kings and priests. They are of the Melchisedec priesthood, able to minister to the Lord, cast their crowns, yet are on thrones like kings ruling. We are looking for elders of cities, ones who will protect the holiness of God and His righteousness. They will protect the redeemed from the accuser of the brethren as well. They will not be every pastor and may possibly only be a few. But this apostolic covering will become the covering for the state. God is weaving a remnant as a single covering in Iowa, whose garment is carrying the priestly sight and sounds.

Rev. 5:8 The elders have harps, golden vials and odors of the prayers of the saints. This describes their function as elders, Melchisedec priests and kings.

Harps --- the stewarding of the sounds of heaven- "Spirit of worship"

Golden Vials – the stewarding of what will be

poured out -"Spirit of Faith"

Odors – Stewarding of the requests or prayers of the saints -"Spirit of Prayer"

Elders are carrying the very song of God in their heart. They are great men and women of faith who have not been moved by opposition or lack of forward advancement because they are carrying the very prayers of the saints in their hearts, waiting for fire to come.

Revelation 8:1–5 (KJV 1900) — 1 And when he had opened the seventh seal, there was silence in heaven about the space of half an hour. 2 And I saw the seven angels which stood before God; and to them were given seven trumpets. 3 And another angel came and stood at the altar, having a golden censer; and there was given unto him much incense, that he should offer it with the prayers of all saints upon the golden altar which was before the throne. 4 And the smoke of the incense, which came with the prayers of the saints, ascended up before God out of the angel's hand. 5 And the angel took the censer, and filled it with fire of the altar, and cast it into the earth: and there were voices, and thunderings, and lightnings, and an earthquake.

There are the three again: Voices are the remnant,

thundering is the prophets and lightening is the apostles. These will be moved by the fire mingled with what they have carried in their hearts, the prayers of the saints. We all are waiting for the fire to come but who has carried the prayers of the saints in their hearts with faith and the song of the Lord?

In ***Rev. 5:9*** a new song is sung, a song of the Lamb, a song of redemption begins to be sung by the elders, then the voice, and the four beasts. It is a song that both connects humanity to heaven and reveals heaven through humanity. The four beasts will release the four breaths found in Ezekiel and begin to move the seven glories into motion. This divine activity of heaven upon earth is done first through the elders and voices. It sets the entire heavenly host into motion.

So this is the beginning of my understanding of building a throne for God in our state. We must find the true elders over cities and regions and let them be released as they are carrying the prayers of the saints in their hearts. We must form gathering places like the Sea of Glass before the throne. We must allow the thunder and lightning to fully have a place as the prophets and apostles will come forth. We must establish a holy community flowing as one with a singular focus on HIM. There will be more to come in the days ahead as the revelation unfolds.

Darrin Begley   May 2015

God is extending your boundaries. Especially in the prophetic decrees that are coming shall have such accuracy, not just for Iowa but for other states because you are beginning to connect. It will become so precise, you will have to put it into the hands of the ones who will know what to do with it and how to release it. God says the accuracy it will have will be at another level. He's going to show you things and it will have a supernatural manifestation. It's going to be so accurate. It is not just for Iowa. As you position yourself, I will show you the state and speak specifically, and you see how it supernaturally connects back to Iowa and the center in which God has you in. God's plan for Iowa is no mixture, I have put you together because there is no mixture, You have a pure heart and I can trust you with the resources I am releasing to you. Not only for your state but others. You connect, there is a reason you are in the middle, you're going to be amazed at how all four directions will connect. You're going to connect different states and relationships. It's going to help break open the apostolic dimension that God has for this nation. Understand how important you are. You cannot pull back because you are vital to the nation. Do not allow the enemy to allow you to be pulled backward. Realize your value.

The Fire Within
Greg Crawford   April 2015

I hear the Lord say, Do not look to those far away to come and ignite the fire. For there will be some that will come and they will begin to ignite some fires, yes, but the fires will be short-lived. There will be some that will come and they will kindle their own flame for their own fire. And pay no heed to those, for those will die out as well. For I will raise up those within this state, says the Lord, that will be carriers of the flame and they will be the ones of fire that will go forth. And they will sustain that which I am about to bring forth into the earth. They have the investment of the land hidden in their heart. And they will sustain that. And they will fight for it, war over it and they will rejoice for it to see it come forth into fullness. So do not heed those that would come from afar, for they will only bring a certain degree of my flame. But I am, even in this hour, raising up those from within, raising them from the very dirt and the dust, says the Lord, to carry the flame.

And when my prophets come in the month of June, they will finalize that which shall be. For you think even in this hour that the new season begins in seven days, but I say it begins even this night. For this night I begin to break forth the new season upon you, says the Lord. And when my prophets come in June they will finalize the season that is now beginning to break forth. And you will come into your destiny and purpose that you have longed for and struggled to understand. Many have even abandoned the destiny and purpose that lies before them thinking it is here or it is there, thinking they can go and be a flame in another place where they have no investment of the land in their heart. But I say unto you, for those who have remained steadfast and faithful, that have endured the shame and the chastisement of many, the ridicule and the rejection of much, I will raise you up to be the messengers of fire and flame and you will sustain that which is about to break forth.

For the next 90 days, I will begin to formulate something in you of great substance and great wealth. Something that has been set aside, placed in your heart, hidden along the way that others have even tried to take and discourage you from seeing. But what I am going to do, says the Lord, no man will stop. And you have seen the beginning of it in other places that have longed for it. And you have heard the reports in other places and regions and said, "Oh God, why can it not be here? Why can it not be us?" And you have allowed the enemy to come and convince you to steal your inheritance from you, to cause you to be in faithlessness. But I say, only believe me, only believe me, only believe me. And I shall cause these things to come, says the Lord, only believe me. Let your doubt and despair be pushed aside. Do not be dismayed. Do not let hopelessness control your heart. Do not let your soul or your mind begin to dictate to your spirit. But let your spirit rise in this hour and see me in new heights and new ways. Let your spirit come before me and I will begin to tell you the mysteries of the kingdom that have been hidden for this age that is now breaking forth. For don't you know the eternal realm is breaking in upon you? And that which is everlasting shall be everlasting and it will remain everlasting even when the temporal has disappeared. For that for which you are laboring and working for is that which is of everlasting, that which is the essence of who I am, the essence of my very being, my Spirit.

And I say unto you, Come, rise. Come and rise and take your places, Mighty Warriors, and as men and women of God that have been chosen for this time and season of the earth. For the assignment that lies before you, for the depths of what it would be. Your understanding does not have to be complete for my Wisdom shall make up the lack. The utterance of my Spirit will give the Breath and it will confront the hearts of men and they will turn in a moment of time. And you will see the wickedness of men's hearts. But you will see the hope of that which is eternal land upon the wickedness in the heart and begin to dissolve it and remove it and cause it to spring forth in a new life.

There are many in this hour that I am pulling and dealing with. And I am looking and longing for the place where people have come after me and my Presence to such a degree that they will not allow anything to hinder their walk or their belief or their understanding of what I could do. I say, because of what I am about to do is bigger than what you have dreamed of, and it is bigger than what you think you can contain, and it is bigger than what you can plan for. For I say there is even coming a season where that which you have as a building and as a place will not contain what I am about to do. No matter how large you begin to grow and build and plan and scheme. For what I do will require you to step out into areas that are not even your very own. And I will cause you to go forth into places people will begin to call and an understanding into why they have called the outcome of what will be in the journey you are about to go on.

And the prophets that come will begin to make known that which is in my heart in a new way. And you will begin to see things and your faith begin to be ignited. And it will pull others in like a big vacuum and a whirlwind. And the fire of the whirlwind will come and it will begin to burn the dross and the chaff out of people's lives. And, even as tonight, out of your very heart there is beginning to be a burning of the chaff that is there that lies within. There's a burning of the dross that has risen to the top and is skimming off. There is coming the refiner's Fire and the Fuller's Soap. And I will cleanse the outside and cleanse that which is within. And there will be purity in my house once again and holiness will be established. For these are the things I am beginning to bring forth in the earth. And this is what will cause the outcast to come. This is what will cause the ones of hopelessness to come because they will see the purity that is upon my people and they will know there is hope once again. They will know there is a God in the earth that is concerned with the affairs and the intentions of men's hearts. There is a God that has answers and I will be the answer for them. It will not be you but it will be me. And I will bring that which is eternal into their heart. And the joy of salvation will begin to spring into the earth once again. And the harvest will come forth and it will not be lost. For it will be brought in, and it will be thrown into the wind, and the chaff will blow away. And the Refiner will come and purify what remains and the end will be.

For I say it is a season, it is a season to call forth that which has not been seen. It is a season to call forth that which you have only dreamed of. It is a season, a season to call forth with the sound of heaven in your voice. It is a season that I shall do things that you have never even dreamed of or thought of or even considered. And I will become your God in a new way, a new and living way, and it will even overtake you at times and you will not know what to do with my Spirit resting upon you except to yield and to give in and say, "Yes, God, here I am. Send me."

For I say, this is a season of something new coming. There are some even in this room, says the Lord. You have not had your encounter with me that has shifted your heart. I say, I am coming for your heart to encounter you that you could encounter me. Just pursue me a little longer. Pursue me a little deeper. Pursue me just a little more and I will come in a very unexpected way. You will see that I have come into your life and the encounter will begin and the understanding will come and Wisdom will set in. For those who will carry this flame will have my Wisdom as their portion. My Wisdom will rest upon sons and daughters. It will rest upon fathers and mothers in new ways.

Apostle Greg –
Prayer - I just break off the woundedness that some are experiencing because of fathering relationships. I break off the tie that has held back people from embracing the fullness of Father God. Healing to come where there has been woundedness.

I hear the Lord say, I can bring encounter to heal the woundedness but I want the woundedness healed so the encounter would be joyful.

Iowa Crossing the Borders
Marty Gabler   June 2015

There is a move of God in His righteous concern for elementary students next year in this state. An intervention. I declare that our children will not be exposed to that which is not righteousness for them to be exposed to. I declare there is a rechecking and a reevaluating and that new blood is coming into the system for curriculum.
Come on Missouri, come on Minnesota.
There is – I saw it earlier, and I saw it again just now – all of the states surrounding Iowa - what do we got 5 or 6? - there is a drawing anointing, some grace of God Almighty in Iowa to draw from the surrounding states. To draw interest, to draw partnership.
It's like I see hands coming over the border into Iowa. It is like I see hands going out of Iowa over the border going into other states. For projects. For effort. For synergy. I declare I am calling for a

synergy of Wisdom. I declare that I am calling for thinking Christians that have a mind. And I am calling for the coming generations: thinkers. You are going to see an increase of intelligent quotient in this state.

There are going to be more students studying college courses while they are still in junior high and high school. I declare to you in this state and in these surrounding states that cross hands for the synergy of God, more and more students that are excelling intellectually and in technology that more and more of them will be fulfilled in a better environment with better curriculum instead of being held back and frustrated. So that they can excel sooner and get into the market place sooner, get into medicine sooner, get into business sooner, get into politics sooner. For the glory of God.

There will be a confrontation with several witches, especially locally. Statewide – covens? – what I am hearing is, it won't be like fighting over beliefs. They have been searching out the spirit realm (there is only one spirit realm). What is happening in the spirit realm, in séances, etc., is not some different experience but they are out there illegally because they are uncovered by the blood of Jesus. All kinds of things can happen. And what will never happen is you will never find fulfillment. And another thing that will never happen is the discovery of truth and The True One, you will be on an endless search.

And the confrontation is going to be, hey, they are ready, they have been searching, they are looking for an answer, you have it, you simply begin to share the truth with them, and they receive.

I am also hearing there is one branch, I don't know, one practice, one denomination of them, whatever you want to call it, that there will be so many people unfulfilled in it that they are going to lose interest in it and that thing is going to shut down.

There is going to be in this region an increase of aging parents accepting Jesus. I am here to tell you, and I am declaring, that there is going to be, we are going to see in this region particularly, an increase of aged parents accepting Jesus Christ.

There will be dealings and conviction of the Holy Spirit concerning elderly abuse and neglect in this region, in this state. And once again, do not forget what was spoken earlier, there needs to be some hands crossing state lines; both ways. For what the Lord is doing. There is going to be legislation to protect the elderly and to provide better services. There is going to be some honoring.

The Lord is saying to our churches and will continue to say in the future to the churches in this region: Churches are no longer to be stablers.

Think about some old Roy Rogers movies, or some old black and white movies, you know.

Think about a stable. I imagine you have a lot of it here too. In the region where we live, and some friends of ours who have ranches and whatnot, they have stables. They board horses. It is really a cool thing out there on the edges of Houston. They have riding stables out there. A city boy and a city gal can play cowboy. They can go buy a horse and can spend all the money they want to, depending on how 'purdy' they want the horse to be, and they buy 'em a horse.

You buy the horse, and you take it out there, and put it in the stable. They'll pet that buggar for you. You don't even have to pet him. They will pet him for you! After all, you are paying so much a month, they ought to floss his teeth for you. Rub his tummy. They will pet that buggar. They will feed him sweet feed. They will feed him alfalfa. They will curry him. Comb him. Every time you go to that stable he will not have one knot in his mane or in his tail. He will always look 'purdy.' They will bathe that buggar for you. They will walk him. Am I describing churches or what? Those horses lo-o-ove it. They will feed them sugar cubes, and they just love it!

More and more churches are going to stop being because they are getting the revelation of the Word of God and the agenda of the Kingdom of God and the advancing of the Kingdom of God and the view of the mature sons of God. And we are going to stop… Rick Joyner said years ago one of the greatest weapons the enemy is going to use against the end-time church is to send needy people into the church so that the leadership and the people use up their attention and their finances on the needy who come in among them. Drain the leadership emotionally.

In spite of whatever you can put in that blank, the Kingdom of God IS advancing! This prophecy of 27,000 in 17 days will come into the kingdom in Iowa… man, that's easy! There ain't nothin' hard about that.

I declare the Kingdom of God is advancing in Polk County. The Kingdom of God is advancing in Iowa. The Kingdom of God is advancing in all these surrounding states. Look out, Minnesota! You cold state, with the cold water lakes. You are going to become a state of Fire and a state of Heat of God. That God is pouring out in His manifestation power. And the Kingdom of God is advancing even though darkness would defy it.

There is a joining of hands for legislation. I do not know how that is going to work. But [there is] a joining together of hands for legislation across state borders between Iowa and Minnesota. Righteous legislation. There are going to be some heads get together and get this thing figured out; under the directive of the Holy Spirit and the principles of the word of God.

I am calling forth members of the House of Representatives of this state and from surrounding states that will under the fear of God encourage, initiate, and support righteous legislation.
I am calling senators forth in the name of Jesus.

I am calling forth high school graduates, college students, and college graduates to the true God, to the Truth of the true God; away from the empty promises of humanism, from the delusion of humanism, and empty philosophies that have no life.

Word for Iowa, Greg Crawford, 2/23/16 Visitation of the Lord for Iowa

The Lord is visiting me very strongly recently in the night. This is the second time this has occurred in the last two months. The first time He spoke to me about the current condition of the Church and showed me the next four years and what the Church would look like. I have not been released to speak of this first visitation. This time again at 2:20 the Lord began to speak to me in a dialogue format for about an hour. At 3:20, He said 'go and write of these things'. This is the highlights I was to write. He explained each point more in-depth than what I have written. I feel released to share the following.

"I indeed am burning the religious cornfields of Iowa as the prophet prophesied just two years ago. I am moving in the fields of Iowa as Ruth moved to glean. This gleaning will first occur in the fields before the suburbs and is just now beginning. The metro areas are still full of themselves and are not in the desperate place of hopelessness as those in the rural areas are. The rural areas spiritual poverty has caused a hunger that has caused a seeking. The city areas are still embracing works and not my graces, embracing the man made ideas and approaches and not the activation of what I have deposited. Works are anything that does not have My graces active. It is what can be attained with or without Me. Graces are what is attained only through Me working first in the heart and then outwardly.

My graces have been deposited and you need to seek them to truly find and know them. My ways are higher than your ways and how I will accomplish My plan will both consume and engulf your thoughts of how you think it will be. But where you find strife, jealousy, contentions and pride, you will find a lack of the Kingdom, a lack of grace being active and a self-satisfaction and contentment. There are many striving to attain and attaining for fame. This has caused a disheartening in my Body. It has become a cancer that begins to consume and weaken My people. It is not the way of advance but is demonic at its root. My way is to be servant of all. My ways are to be in a constant state of humility.

It is indeed a season of My kingdom being seen, being felt, and being heard. But the resistance My prophets and apostles are feeling is a resistance to their voice, as it is a voice of My Kingdom representation. Men want my prophets and apostles present in their meetings to affirm themselves, but do not want to hear their voice and resist hearing their voice. By resisting my apostles and prophets, they are resisting My Kingdom and even at times, opposing Me. Thus the undealt with pride in men's hearts is keeping them from My Kingdom and has caused a spirit of pride to be placed as a ruling one over cities. But this pride in men's hearts has created a gulf of pride between alignment of heaven and earth. It has caused Me to resist many of the efforts of men. It had caused me to hold away at arm's length.

I have positioned My servants in this hour, hidden yet known, full of wisdom, yet denied voice. I have placed them and have moved upon their hearts with long patience, forming them for this moment of time. A remnant voice. As they begin to come forth in the new season they are entering, they will do so with words that will cut the spiritual atmosphere and divide even the seas that stop the advance of My people into what I have promised. My people are carrying My promises but the structures they have associated with are stopping them from seeing what they know to be true in their hearts. I am coming to change many structures, I am coming to remove some structures, and I am coming to birth My original structure and its intentions.

Think it not odd what you have carried all these years as My forerunners and pioneers as not being able to be completed. But look now as this is the season for what was conceived will come forth. It will spring forth as a new dew dropping down upon the earth. A residue of heaven itself with a fragrance of My presence. It will cover many like a mantle and by its touch many will be set free and mantled. Even in this hour I am re-mantling many. Some men have created their own mantle but do not take heed to it as when My mantle is seen, it will also be felt. This new mantling will cause a great clarity and awakening in the heart to occur. In 'a suddenly', a single moment of time, all confusion will be gone, all divide in the heart will be touched.

I am bringing forth both the means to attain the harvest of the fields and also the means of the harvest. I am beginning a dealing in the hearts of many. For some, they have already been in that place. For others, their journey is beginning and still others will miss the moment, caught up in what they have created. But nonetheless, I will have My way and the plans of men and the schemes of the enemy and the wiles of the demonic will not be able to resist what I am about to do. It will be like a giant wave crashing ashore and all of these things many thought they were powerless over and victims of, they will see swept into My sea of forgetfulness for these things are nothing for Me.

For this is the year of My sons and daughters. They are coming forth as sent by Me for Me to manifest Me, not themselves. They will come forth a fresh fragrance on the land, restorers of the breach, attainers of the golden victory. They will march and not grow faint. They will decree with only a desire to please Me. They will not look at men's faces in fear, but look at men's hearts in seeing how to unlock the hidden treasure."

Iowa – Iona / Apostolic Hub
Brian Hume   Sept 2017

Brian Francis Hume had a dream in 2006 concerning Iowa that he shared in 2017. In the dream, he was at a prayer meeting with Kirk Bennett, and Kirk was holding a piece of paper with "IOWA" written on it he watched the "IOWA" change to "IONA" and knew that Iowa is to become an Iona. Along with this dream, he briefly stated Iowa would be known as an apostolic hub.

What's interesting is that I talked about this word about four months prior to him releasing while in Iowa. The subject that I spoke on was Righteousness and the oil of Gladness. Iona, an island in the Hebrides, considered the most Holy Island where St Columba established a monastery and launched missions to Scotland and Great Britain. The Hebrides have experienced several significant events over the years. Iona became the base of Irish Christian missionary St Columba, who in 563 AD landed on the island with twelve followers and settled there. He was looked upon as being a pioneering Christian taking the gospel of the Kingdom to Scotland and Great Britain from this small insignificant island. Though it was small in size, the impact that came from this hidden place was large and felt by many.

Interestingly it became a place of advance learning and publishing documents that were thought to be sourced of the early Irish Annals. The Monastery was known to practice Celtic Christianity and the Celtic cross with the ring in the middle originated from this island.

This word has many different prophetic significances. First, being hidden, second, being small but having great influences. This is part of the pattern the words for Iowa have been. The concept of an apostolic hub has been modeled in Iowa by the BASE for almost 20 years and is prevalent in other areas. Part of apostolic hubs is the teaching dynamic, writing of documents, sending outward on mission. These hubs are also places of influence in the spiritual realm and then in the earth. They carry and create environments not found in traditional settings thus they are able to activate people into giftings and destinies.

Greg Crawford

ABOUT THE AUTHOR

Greg Crawford has been active in ministry for over 30 years serving in almost every type of leadership role. He is the founder of Jubilee International Ministries, which has birthed Jubilee School of Ministry a fully accredited school operating for 15 years with international students, an online school and Jubilee International School of Ministry which grew to over 50+ schools in developing nations, graduating roughly 6,000 students yearly. He has also planted Jubilee Kingdom Gathering an apostolic church and currently oversees "The BASE" an apostolic Kingdom Center in the Iowa state capital to bring awakening and reformation. The forerunner ministry of the BASE has creative spontaneous worship, gift and call development, investment by spiritual fathering and revelatory instruction with opportunity, and points of influences. The BASE holds state wide Awakening meetings several times a year where people from across the state attend.

Apostle Crawford or APG as he is

known by many, has traveled on numerous international trips, leading teams into nations conducting leadership conferences. He has worked in Cote D' Voire, Nigeria, South Africa, Zambia, and Indonesia. He laid the ground work for the apostolic reformation in Nigeria and gives counsel to numerous ministries and leaders connected with Him. He serves on the board of Midwest Christian Center, and is the apostolic covering for several churches and Kingdom Centers.

Apostle Crawford has become a spiritual father and has labored to see the Kingdom expression of awakening by travels in Iowa and the United States to help bring this into existence. He is best known for his revelatory teaching style and has a unique and powerful ministry of laying on of hands for impartation. This has opened the door for him to speak at many national conferences. The revelatory dynamic is reflected in the many books he has written available on Amazon and Kindle.

He holds a PHD of Ministry which he received Magna Suma Cum Laude. He is ordained with Jim Hodges' Federation of

Ministries and Churches International and is in relationship with several well known national voices. More information can be found at the ministry website **www.thebaseiowa.org**

For More information contact

"The Base"

Des Moines, Iowa

www.thebaseiowa.org

Greg Crawford